UNDERSTANDING
MALE AUTHORITY

IT WAS NEVER ABOUT PRIDE AND ALWAYS ABOUT HUMILITY

UNDERSTANDING
MALE AUTHORITY

IT WAS NEVER ABOUT PRIDE AND ALWAYS ABOUT HUMILITY

LAMBERT SANDS

ISBN (hc) ISBN-10: 0-9911546-6-5
ISBN-13: 978-0-9911546-6-1
ISBN (e): 978-0-9911546-7-8

Printed in the United States of America
Marriage Mechanics Ministries, Inc. 08/15/2020

"WISDOM IS THE PRINCIPAL THING; THEREFORE GET WISDOM: AND WITH ALL THY GETTING GET UNDERSTANDING."

– PROVERBS 4:7

FOREWORD

BY DR. MILES MUNROE

One of the greatest challenges of the 21st century is the gender war. Never before in history has the lines between male and female been so gray. During the last century the fight for equality between the male and female gender has taken conflict to another level. This declaration of the females' right to participate in social, political and economic processes in societies throughout the world has created a new equation for the value of the sexes in our post-modern society.

The historical biblical record of the creation of the male and female and the establishment of the divine relations structure between them as seen in the Holy Scriptures is clear. However, nowhere has there been more controversy over this issue than in the religious world. Churches, mosques, and synagogues have been the battleground for this conflict and many are still not sure the war is over. However, it is important to remember that no one knows the gender product like the Manufacturer and therefore when there is confusion about the functioning of a product we should refer to the Manufacturer's manual.

In this work, "Understanding Male Authority," Lambert Sands takes the reader back to the foundation of the relationship between male and female. His simple, profound style leaps over the complicated theological boundaries to open the Word and reveal the principles of manhood and the role and responsibilities of the male. His candid approach to the subject is just what men and women need to overcome the confusing alternatives of cultural and social pressure. I believe that this book will become a classic and should be read by all women and the men that love them. I challenge you to dive into these pages and let the power, truth and practical principles transform your concept and attitude of the male role in relationships and in life.

Dr. Miles Munroe

ACKNOWLEDGMENTS

We must always remember that whatever wisdom we have, it comes from the Lord. He gave me the grace to complete this work. I am grateful and humbled that He would allow me to speak to His people. I am also thankful to the many people who assisted in bringing this work to fruition. Mike Valentino, Verona Missick, and Kevin Downs did a tremendous job editing and clearing out my numerous grammatical errors. Julie Csizmadia produced a very thought-inspiring cover. Special thanks to the late Dr. Myles Munroe who was gracious in many ways. He assisted Kim and me by providing editing services for our TV program at the Diplomat Center in the Bahamas. He also wrote a foreword for this book as well as "The Power of Submission."

I am grateful to my son and daughters: Lambert Jr., Krysta Ashleah and Kayla who have been pillars of strength after the passing of Kim, my late wife of twenty-seven years. Without her and them, this work would have been much impeded.

TABLE OF CONTENTS

INTRODUCTION

When I started to write this book, I thought that I knew what masculine authority or authority in general really meant. Little did I know that this book would change my life and my perception of authority forever. I now revere the very word authority, knowing the awesome responsibility that those in leadership carry. Like Adam, every male has been delegated authority by God to be a custodian of His earth.

Sadly, the custodial keys to divine authority have been lost in our apostate times. Most men are in a coma, knocked out in the tenth round by a clever and superior opponent. Dazed and oblivious to what is going on around them, the enemy has moved in for the kill. Exposed and unprotected, wives and children are confused and in bondage to lies and deception. Society and communities have become bastions of violence and crude ungodly behavior; all because the male role has been vacated.

However, all is not lost. The Lord is still calling! Like the day Adam lost authority in the Garden of Eden, the Lord is calling men back to Him; back to a place where they can find real power and wisdom to overcome their most elusive and clever foe. Lacking wisdom and the power of God, men are beating the air thinking that the enemy is their wives, the government or some ungodly organization.

This lack of perception is precisely why men continue to lose the war against evil. For men to recover what they have lost and defeat the enemy, they must undress. They must shed the garments of pride and arrogance. They must return to the Master's feet and learn. My prayer for every man that reads this book is true repentance. The Lord has not changed. We have.

We have turned from grace and mercy to do our own thing. Now, the enemy has gained the edge and our only hope is the Lord. Our only solution is to uncover the forgotten principles that bring God's grace. As you turn the pages of this book, let the mercy and grace of God open your eyes to see and understand truth that would usher you into a new realm of authority.

Lambert Sands

WHO AM I?

INTRODUCTION

If you don't know who you are, there is always someone willing to define you. Sadly, during our time, the voices of social media and the news media have redefined truth, integrity and moral standards. People are inclined to listen to what they see and hear on TV or the internet. They would rather listen to what the masses say rather than follow the beaten but often forbidden pathway to truth. As our Lord said, *"Enter ye in at the strait gate: for wide is the gate, and broad is the way, that leadeth to destruction, and many there be which go in thereat: Because strait is the gate, and narrow is the way, which leadeth unto life, and few there be that find it." (Matthew 7:13-14)*

Understanding your purpose is perhaps one of the most profound teachings of our time. We must answer the questions: who am I and why am I here? Like an instructor once said to me, *"You are not who people say you are, you are not even who you think you are, you are what God's word says you are."* There are a lot of voices claiming gender knowledge but their claims have not led to healing or marriage and family unity. They started a war; a war designed to destroy the family.

Like Adam, men are again mishandling authority because of ignorance. And, the stakes could not be any higher. Civilization is teetering on the brink of disaster. The question: will the male man get back in his God ordained and God called position?

CHAPTER 1

THE AWAKENING

The siren was blaring in my ears. I was sitting beside the pastor's wife who was telling me that everything was going to be okay. But why was I in the back of an ambulance? And who was the bloodied white male lying motionless and breathing heavily under the oxygen mask? "Brother Sands...your car collided with his."

Turning to the man, whom I had never seen before, I prayed for him. It was a reflective action. I was in a daze and operating in auto-mode. *Did I get married?* Sister Alleyne, the pastor's wife, smiled but didn't reply. She rubbed my shoulder instead.

When the ambulance reached the hospital, I was quickly ushered into an emergency room. "How many fingers do I have up?"

"Three," I replied.

"And what year is it?"

"I honestly don't know," I replied.

The doctor had a concerned look on his face as he pressed heavily on several parts on my body asking if I felt pain. "No, just my arm hurts a little."

After further examination, the doctor sounded relieved to tell me that I was okay, and I could go home but I should be monitored for any change.

I was happy to know my good prognosis, but I had lost almost a year of information! I was suffering from temporary amnesia. The accident had knocked information out of my head. I had only been married a month. That information was gone. I knew Kim (my wife) but I couldn't remember that we were married. That night we slept in the same bed...in faith!

If you have never experienced amnesia, you won't understand this experience. You just can't remember "stuff." You can't connect to facts that are supposed to be in your memory bank. **Information and facts can be staring you right in the face and you cannot comprehend them.** You are in a trance unable to properly relate to what is happening. Wow! Today, sad to say, most men are in this predicament: In a deep sleep, unable to respond properly to what is happening around them.

A cunning and crafty enemy has knocked us into a coma. And, before we can assume our God-called position, we must understand who we are, and what we are called to do. You see, we were created with awesome power and ability to rule the world. Power that was lost the day Adam sinned in Eden. It took me some time to get my memory back, and it will take time for men to understand and walk in their God-ordained authority. It started in Eden, and that is where we must return to understand God's purpose for men and what went wrong.

WHO AM I?

The hovering bright light was the first thing that Adam saw when he opened his eyes. The brilliant light enveloped his naked body, giving him alternating sensations of joy, peace and love. All at once, he knew who he was and why God had created him. His name was Adam and God had created him to govern the Earth. Lying down on the ground, spiritual knowledge flowed through his mind and heart like a rushing river cascading over the banks of a high fall. He was aware of God and the world that God had created for him.

The days and weeks after his creation, Adam's spiritual growth progressed unabated. Daily, God would visit him and commune with him, spiritually empowering him with divine knowledge to govern his environment. God continued to assign him more duties. First, he was given the chore of keeping and dressing of Eden. Then, he was given the task of naming the animals. Everything seemed to be going well and God was pleased with his progress.

Now, Adam was ready for his final test of authority. God had placed within Adam at creation, a rib, female DNA that would soon become his wife, the best thing that he could ever have. Then the day finally came. While Adam lay asleep under the anesthesia of the Holy Spirit, God painlessly removed the embryo DNA and made Eve. Together, they were to govern the earth. It was pure ecstasy for both as they played and romanced inside the confines of Eden. Little did they know that in a few months, they would be kicked out of their garden paradise and introduced to a life of pain and suffering.

The Bible says that God created man (meaning mankind) in His own image and likeness. Both male and female represent the invisible God. Genesis 1:27, "So God created <u>man (mankind) in his own image</u>, in the image of God created he him; male and female created he them." For those who thought that God is a man, (meaning male man) {Brackets mine}…think again. God is neither a male nor a female. **He is a spirit.** However, He has chosen to reveal His attributes *differently* through the male and female gender. The purpose of this book is to isolate the male role or male side of God as best as I can.

Adam, the male, was created first. This is significant. He was created first for a specific purpose. He was the one designated with senior authority and leadership. Thus, he became ***responsible*** for the spiritual atmosphere of the whole world. The days and weeks before Eve was created were for the sole purpose of education; Adam needed to understand and flow in his role, or better, let God flow through him. God did this by assigning him tasks. He was to be a caretaker of the Garden of Eden. We don't know exactly what that entailed, however, when God cursed the ground, He said, "*…thorns also and thistles shall it bring forth to thee; and thou shalt* *eat the herb of the field." (Genesis 3:18)* From this we can surmise that Adam's task may have included landscaping and gardening.

He was also given the task of naming the animals *and eventually named his wife.* But, how did he learn to do all this? Did it just come to him? Did he ponder and then come to a conclusion about what to do? No, and a million times no. Adam was created pure, meaning without sin. **When Adam came off the product line God could freely fellowship with him.** This is an awesome statement!!

You see, God is authority and the source of every power behind the universe. God also has all knowledge and all wisdom. God is behind nature. He is behind gravity and every other law that we use to gauge and measure the universe. In fact, He holds everything together by His word. When He created man, He created him to walk in this authority. Wow! And Adam did just that. The wisdom of God flowed through Adam like a river. He understood how to take care of Eden. He knew what to call the animals. Don't the names lion, tiger, dog, eagle, raven, dove fit the creatures more than sophisticated scientific names like *Felis Concolor* – a mountain lion or *Castor Canadensisor* – a beaver?

My brother, God has designated you to walk in divine authority. He wants you to walk in the supernatural to sense His voice and know what He wants you to do. **This is your purpose: To use authority to uphold all that is good.** This is the authority that Adam gave up when he sinned. **This is the authority Satan resists.** He knows if you truly understand who you are, and the authority that God has made available to you, his goose is cooked in your life. When a man walks in authority, he can bring deliverance to his family.

When a man walks in divine authority, the wisdom of God is made available to him. He becomes a better lover to his wife because he understands her feminine needs. He sees through the cloud of human behavior and can make wise decisions based not on mere rational thought, but according to the wisdom of God's Spirit, which, by the way, is usually contrary to human thought. *"Trust in the LORD with all thine heart; and lean not unto thine own understanding. In all thy ways acknowledge him, and he shall direct thy paths. Be not wise in thine own eyes: fear the LORD, and depart from evil." (Proverbs 3:6-7)*

AUTHORITY LOST

When Adam disobeyed the voice of God by eating from the fruit of Good and Evil, he aligned himself with Satan: the spirit of rebellion or the **my-way** spirit. Adam compromised his position of authority by following his wife in rebellion against the word of God. He compromised his authority to appease his wife. Indeed, it takes faith and confidence to obey the word of God when everybody else is doing their own thing. It's easy to suck up to people so we are not the odd one out. **<u>But compromise is the spirit of the coward who is fearful and afraid to tackle and confront challenges.</u>**

Always, and in every way, the question will be: Will we obey the word of faith or continue to take matters into our own hands? Will we listen to the voice of God or be dominated by our fears? The first sin was compromise and fear of rejection, which leads to selfish, self-centered decisions. Adam chose himself over loving God, and fear of losing Eve over gaining God's approval. For a moment, just a moment, Adam forgot who he was and what his purpose was. *He allowed Satan to cause him to give up his authority through compromise.*

This is the deadly sin that plagues most men; leaders and all who must bear the burden of responsibility. Will they compromise to appease or will they stand for the truth of God? Will they use their authority for selfish means, or to further the plans of Almighty God? You see, authority is God's means of establishing order, keeping peace and fulfilling His will. Whether it is within the family or a nation, God uses authority to fulfill His will. Thus, God commissioned Adam to "keep" the garden. He was to use his authority to fulfill God's purposes.

This deadly sin of compromise can be seen throughout the Bible, where men instead of standing in authority in obedience to God, compromised for one reason or another to please either their own flesh or the flesh of others: whether it was wife, children, friends or countrymen. However, their sin not only affected them but their families and their nations. For Adam, his sin affected all mankind. He was the first representative of God's authority on earth. And what he did, would determine the fate of mankind. Whether a life of perpetual peace, harmony, and physical abundance, or sorrow, pain, and labor.

THE HIDING PLACE

Adam botched God's highest hope for mankind. He further compounded the predicament in which he found himself by hiding. He *misunderstood* the heart of God and hid himself from the only person who could help him. This is now the tragedy of fallen mankind and the male man. He refuses to go to God. *He refuses to submit to the Lord's authority and spends his entire life making mistake after mistake.* You see, God has a will for mankind. He has a will for every man and woman on the planet. And just as the angels in heaven fulfill His every purpose, His perfect plan is for every man and woman to daily do the same.

When we hide from our mistakes or from taking authority, it means that we are not properly connected to the source and we cannot see spiritually to make the right decisions. Like Adam, who was afraid to approach God after he had sinned, when we live far from God, we are unsure of His intentions or His plans for us. We believe the lies of Satan and his cohorts. Sadly, most men live in this insecurity and fear that cause them to cower rather than to stand up to the deceptions of Satan.

Defeated men put on a mask of pride or exhibit a false sense of strength to cover their fears and insecurities. They pretend that they have it all together but when they are put to the test, they compromise. Story after story is told in the Bible of men, who instead of standing firm in their position of authority, compromised to appease others.

Adam, Abraham, Lot, Saul, Eli the priest, all tasted the sour grapes of appeasement. They disobeyed God's word and His revelation to them to please someone else. In each case, instead of referring to God and what

God said, they listened to the devious and rebellious voice of self; the area where Satan controls and hides in our lives.

Abraham's mistake is a classic example of compromise. After years of no children, his wife, Sarah, decided to help God succeed. She told Abraham to copulate with her maid, Hagar, and, thus, they would fulfill the plan of God. Instead of seeking God's opinion through prayer and waiting on God's reply, Abraham went ahead with his wife's plan. Abraham got his son, Ishmael, but this was not God's choice. Alas, this man-made plan would not only cause Abraham heartache when he had to send Ishmael away when Isaac, the child of promise, was eventually born, it also brought hatred, envy, and eventually war between the Jews and the ancestors of Ishmael which exists even to this day!

We must never hide or disengage ourselves from taking or standing in our position of righteous authority in our homes, or wherever we have been given a position of authority. If we fail to do this and do something else, that is called compromise. It brought death to the human race then and will continue to bring death and destruction until men and those who hold authority stand for truth and justice.

The world itself is in the grip of fear and insecurity. Goliath looks too strong. Facing the mountain of fear looks impossible. But I'm here to tell every man that all the power in the universe is waiting to be released into your spirit. The door is now open for all who want to walk in true authority. All it takes is a willing and obedient spirit.

Hiding means fear and insecurity. Adam hid because he was not sure whether God would accept him back as a friend after he had sinned. He did not know God well enough to understand the heart of a father who only wants the son to acknowledge his sin and total dependency on the father. Yes, there would be consequences for his mistake. *However, God still wanted to fellowship with him and would one day die for this "sin" of mankind.*

CHAPTER 2

WALKING IN DIVINE AUTHORITY

In 1991, my wife and I and moved into our new home. We had lived in an apartment after we got married and this was a welcomed change. We were overjoyed over this latest accomplishment. However, shortly thereafter, the strife and bickering started: arguments about finances and who is really in charge, and as usual I pulled rank. "I'm the man around here and you do what I tell you..." But that only escalated the conflicts. One day after a heated exchange, I went into the bedroom and prayed one of the strangest prayers. Looking back, I know it had to be... the Holy Spirit.

I confessed before God that I was the blame, and took full responsibility. I wept before Him and asked His forgiveness and direction. Shortly after I had finished praying, my wife came into the bedroom. She was different, her attitude of defiance was gone, and from that moment I knew that our marriage would survive this hump. But what had brought about this sudden change? And would it continue?

Like I said, I didn't know why I prayed as I did. Apparently, God had stepped into my prayer life and even in my ignorance, helped me. You see, our problems are never with just humans alone. Our real enemy is Satan, the god of this world. He is the deceiver. He is the marriage destroyer. He is the resister of truth and justice. Jesus said that "the thief cometh to kill, steal and destroy but I have come to bring life." Without the wisdom of God, Satan can outfox and outmaneuver us. Like Jesus, who always walked in victory, we must depend completely on the Holy Spirit.

When I argued with my wife, I was depending on self. It was pride that made me say, "I'm the man." *"Only by pride cometh contention: but with the well advised is wisdom." (Proverbs 13:10)* For most men, we have been brought up in a society that glorifies pride (the devil's world). A society that tells us that being the first and the best is life's aim. A society that says that being superior is right. But, when we move in pride, we wander further and further away from the power and wisdom of God.

However, like I related in my personal experience, as I yielded myself to God, there came a divine flow of authority, and we experienced an immediate change in our home. Humility is one of the greatest demonstrations of faith. ___When a person humbles himself before God, he becomes a candidate for God's awesome power.___ *"If my people which are called by my name, **shall humble themselves** and pray, and seek my face, and turn from their wicked ways; then will I hear from heaven, and will **forgive their sin, and will heal their land."** (2 Chronicles 7:14)* "**Humble yourselves** therefore under the mighty hand of God, that he may **exalt you in due time."** (1 Peter 5:6)* "When pride cometh, then cometh shame: **but with the lowly is wisdom.**" (Proverbs 11:2)*

__Humility is the key to divine authority, and the key to heavenly resources.__ It's the missing dimension in the lives of most men (and most people in general) as they struggle through life making prideful, arrogant, and self-centered decisions. In contrast, the door of humility looks dull and foolish; it looks plain and drab, it looks uninviting; but it is the only way to the favor of God and power of God. It is the key to truly walking in the awesome position of masculine authority. The power of God, the power that can move mountains, is activated by humility. *"__The sacrifices of God are a broken spirit: a broken and a contrite heart, O God, thou wilt not despise.__" (Psalm 51:17)* "For all those things hath mine hand made, and all those things have been, saith the LORD: __but to this man will I look,__* _even to him that is poor and of a contrite spirit, and trembleth at my word." (Isaiah 66:2)_

Humility is like a giant magnet that draws the awesome power of God. Most families today are struggling because husbands and fathers are walking in pride. Without genuine humility and keen spiritual insight, most men cannot flow in the blessing of God.

But what does humility really look like? Is it the spirit of the dutiful or go-for man who obeys every whim of his wife and kids? Is it the self-righteous spirit who does all the good moral things? Again, we have to go back to the perfect image of Christ. What was He like? How did He portray humility? The Bible says that though He was the Son of God, **yet learned he obedience** by the things that He suffered (Hebrews 5). Humility is the maturity of submission and obedience. Jesus' every move, with every fiber of His being, was simply to please God; not people, not religious traditions, not His own will, but the will of the Father.

Humility means we are dedicated to God and unctionized by the Holy Spirit. It calls for **sensitivity** and determination, gentleness and also confrontation. In Jesus, we saw tenderness but He preached fire and brimstone messages. We saw compassion, yet He sharply rebuked the religious leaders of His day. We saw a man run from the praise and accolades of people, yet one who was perfectly secure in who He was. In other words, humility cannot be manufactured; God has to produce humility in us as we learn to obey Him, even in the most trying circumstances.

This requires faith and patience, and an attitude that is totally dependent on God. God chooses our course, we ask Him for faith and patience to stay the course. The Bible says before honor there must be humility. However, for most men, the Devil has put up roadblocks in their minds about their authority. When they think of authority, they usually think of commanding power over people: having people obey their wishes and commands. This is not God's image of authority! God's authority is servant-hood and ministry. _"Ye know that the princes of the gentiles exercise dominion over them, and they that are great exercise authority upon them._

But it shall not be so among you, but whosoever will be great among you, let him be your minister. And whosoever will be chief among you, let him be your servant; Even as the Son of man came not to be ministered unto but to minister and to give his life a ransom for many." (Matthew 20:25-28)

Another way of looking at this is recognizing that at best, your position of authority is transparent. Transparency comes when a man acknowledges that his authority is delegated. His authority has been given in order that he can be an earthly conduit of God's power flow to his family. He is not the final authority, God is. Therefore, his leadership and authority must be tempered with godly meekness. Follow this carefully. Meekness does *not* mean that a man is passive. Meekness means that he is broken before God. He is like the powerful stallion that has been broken by its master, and responds to the faintest movement of the reins. This is the epitome of true leadership and delegated authority.

Meekness was the trademark of great men like Abraham, Moses and the Lord Himself who said, *"For I am meek and lowly…"* Without meekness, leadership will degenerate into fleshly control and coercion. Meekness opens the door for the Spirit of God to direct the man. He can deny himself and allow God to channel through him, the flow of wisdom and spiritual perception that his family needs. The Apostle Paul discovered that when he was weak (weak in his own strength) he was most strong. (2 Corinthians 12:8-10)

I remember a particular time, praying and asking God for wisdom to direct my home, and the Marriage Mechanics Ministries. Each time I prayed, the Holy Spirit stopped me. I felt myself being constrained. Why, I questioned God? Was not this a valid prayer? God told me I did not understand; I was still thinking in the natural, I was still on the surface with regard to His manifold wisdom. But after a few days, He revealed His wisdom to me. "It is delegated authority; your authority comes through Me. You must *allow the authority to **flow** through you.* You must allow Me to do the work through you. You must die to self. Self is that un-crucified area of your life that will use the authority for ungodly means."

You see, I was still thinking as a natural person thinks, that the wisdom and knowledge that they have is to be used as they deem fit. But God wants His people to die completely to self and allow Him to channel His glory through them. The Apostle Paul puts it this way, *"I am crucified with Christ: nevertheless I live; yet not I, but Christ liveth in me: and the life which I now live in the flesh I live by the faith of the Son of God, who loved me, and gave himself for me." (Galatians 2:20)*

This is where men go wrong. This is where most leaders go wrong. They assume that since they have been appointed to a particular position, that justifies their use of authority as they see fit. Or, God's anointing on my life justifies all of my decisions. This is simply not God's way. God's way is *"I and the Father are one."* (John 10:31) In other words, He flows through me unhindered. A man must learn that self-denial is not an option but his only path to true freedom and abundant flow in the Spirit. He must learn to be quiet and allow the Spirit to speak through him. Then and only then will the words he speaks produce the powerful changes in his family that he desires.

AUTHORITY AND THE WIFE

"AND GOD SAID, LET US MAKE MAN IN OUR IMAGE, AFTER OUR LIKENESS: AND LET THEM HAVE DOMINION OVER THE FISH OF THE SEA, AND OVER THE FOWL OF THE AIR, AND OVER THE CATTLE, AND OVER ALL THE EARTH, AND OVER EVERY CREEPING THING THAT CREEPETH UPON THE EARTH. SO GOD CREATED MAN IN HIS OWN IMAGE, IN THE IMAGE OF GOD CREATED HE HIM; MALE AND FEMALE CREATED HE THEM." (GENESIS 1:26-27)

"AND THE LORD GOD SAID, IT IS NOT GOOD THAT THE MAN SHOULD BE ALONE, I WILL MAKE HIM AN HELP MEET FOR HIM. (GENESIS 2:18)

"AND ADAM GAVE NAMES TO ALL CATTLE, AND TO THE FOWL OF THE AIR, AND TO EVERY BEAST OF THE FIELD: BUT FOR ADAM THERE WAS NOT FOUND AN HELP MEET FOR HIM.

AND THE LORD GOD CAUSED A DEEP SLEEP TO FALL UPON
ADAM, AND HE SLEPT: AND HE TOOK OUT ONE OF HIS RIBS,
AND CLOSED UP THE FLESH INSTEAD THEREOF; AND THE RIB,
WHICH THE LORD GOD HAD TAKEN FROM MAN, MADE HE A
WOMAN, AND BROUGHT HER UNTO THE MAN. AND ADAM SAID,
THIS IS NOW BONE OF MY BONES, AND FLESH OF MY FLESH:
SHE SHALL BE CALLED WOMAN BECAUSE SHE WAS TAKEN
OF MAN. THEREFORE SHALL A MAN LEAVE HIS FATHER AND
HIS MOTHER, AND SHALL CLEAVE UNTO HIS WIFE: AND THEY
SHALL BE ONE FLESH. AND THEY WERE BOTH NAKED, THE MAN
AND HIS WIFE, AND WERE NOT ASHAMED." (GENESIS 2:20-25)

Before the fall, both man and woman were unified in their obedience to God. They walked in obedience and unity through the *empowerment of the Holy Spirit. The Holy Spirit was the key to their unity and relationship. This is God's perfect plan.* As we move forward toward the coming of the Lord, and His heavenly kingdom, the relationship between a husband and wife has to become more like God's perfect plan where the genders walk together in divine unity, both humbly doing His will. Let me explain.

It was never about exalting the man, or exalting the woman. It was always about doing God's will and displaying His masculine and feminine attributes. To God be all the glory forever and ever, amen. Man and woman were created to glorify God. They were never to live for themselves, but to live to please Him, first. They did this before the fall.

However, after the fall, sin and rebellion entered the human race. Thus, mankind would now need external codes of ethics to govern their lives. God stated to the woman *"her desire would be to the husband and he would rule over her."* This was to keep her flesh in check, and punishment for overstepping God's ordained authority, and not because she was any less or inferior to the man spiritually. Both man and woman are equal before God, however, there is, and always will be, order in God's kingdom.

God created your wife to be your helpmeet. This means she has been divinely created to assist you to fulfill your mission on earth. She has strengths where you are weak. Learn to listen to her advice, especially in areas where you may be failing. Many men reap bitter results because they fail to listen. On the other hand, you can enjoy the blessing of a prudent wife *if you listen instead of trying to dominate and control her.*

Release her unto the Lord and allow God to bring about godly submission in her life. To demand or coerce your wife to submit to your authority is not only counterproductive, it's ungodly and a gross exploitation of authority. Submission must be offered willingly. Have faith in God! He is very involved and interested in bringing divine order to your home, but it must be done His way: through the power of the Holy Spirit.

My wife and I were brought up in a very strict church background. The church that we attended taught against the wearing of jewelry as an ornament (using 1 Timothy 2:9 and 1 Peter 3:3). However, over the years the "Jewelry for Ornament" teaching was revised and relaxed allowing members to wear jewelry in moderation. There was much confusion concerning the issue. I opted to stick to the old way. So, every time my wife would put on jewelry, I would advise her against it. But daily I heard a voice within saying, "Release your wife, release your wife..." Finally, I obeyed and my wife started to wear earrings and bracelets. However, after several years of doing so, she confessed that indeed the Apostles' word concerning outward adornment was neither cultural nor contemporaneous to its time. She said that there was always a temptation to put on more and more. Now she has developed a discipline to keep the jewelry to a minimum.

Suppose I had not listened to the voice of the Holy Spirit. My wife would still be in bondage to law and would not come to the greater understanding of grace and wisdom through the power of the Holy Spirit. Let me give you another example, let's say you have requested your wife to do something for you, or she may be neglectful or derelict in performance of her duties as a wife. When you bring it to her attention, she resists you or fails to cooperate. Or, she may resist your decision on a certain financial matter. The fleshly and carnal response is usually anger or becoming argumentative. This only compounds the situation. The spiritual response, however, will bring the best result. Remain calm and continue to love her. Remember God has everything under control. You must rely on Him to show you the source of the problem. Could it be she doesn't understand or may be afraid of where the family is going? Take time to reassure her. Patiently wait for her to get the message or accept the idea you are trying to get across.

If she out-rightly defies you, let God handle the situation. Don't take matters into your own hands, this will prove devastating to your marriage. Always respond with love. Being a roughrider shows immaturity and insensitivity. Being right doesn't have to mean being harsh. There will be times and circumstances, when the Holy Spirit will direct you to move forward, regardless of your wife's wishes. However, be sensitive to her feelings and patient with her misunderstandings.

Are there times when a man must submit to his wife? In a technical sense, a man should never subject himself to his wife, this is totally contrary to God's word because the authority of God flows through him. However, a man must submit himself to the word of God and the Spirit of God. When his wife is in sync with God and operating under the influence of the Holy Spirit, a man would do well to heed her words. By doing so he demonstrates humility and the proper understanding of authority. She has been designed to help him. But this still does not change the position of husband or wife.

A good example of this can be seen in Genesis 21, when Sarah the godly wife of Abraham advised him to send away his son born to him by his mistress Hagar. Abraham was very distraught that his wife had asked him to do this and refused. But later he was told by God to hearken unto her voice. Why? She was speaking God's will. The key in these circumstances is to be so spiritually in tune that you can discern when your wife is speaking God's word and giving good advice. Both men and women are required to obey God in everything. However, in the normal flow of authority in the home, a man is required to listen to his wife and to obey God. Conversely, a woman is required to obey her husband in everything as long as it is not against God's word. If he asks his wife to steal, she has a right to disobey. This does not mean that he sticks his wife in a small corner and runs the house himself. He should listen attentively to her suggestions and allow her to aid him.

Male authority was given for man to be a custodian of God's world. It was never given for man to create his own world and install himself as king. For a man to operate in the fullness of authority, he must submit himself unreservedly to Jesus Christ. When a man does this, he will find the glory that created the universe. He will find the power that controls the atom. He will know God. God is power and authority.

CHAPTER 3

PASSIVITY: THE LEADERSHIP KILLER

I think one of the biggest mistakes that I have ever made was a result of my passivity. We were married almost ten years when Kim became pregnant with our fourth child. Before the baby was born, my wife suggested that she should have her fallopian tubes tied (Tubal Ligation). We had both come from families of four children, and it seemed the natural thing to have four of our own.

But the overwhelming reason for the Tubal Ligation was the anxiety and pride that we would look foolish and naïve having another child. At this time in our country, it was becoming a shame for a person even if they were married to have a large family. I loved my wife and I didn't want her to endure the constant anxiety and fear that she would become pregnant again, so I agreed to the Tubal Ligation.

Our obstetrician, who had initially agreed to do the procedure, later tried without success to dissuade us several times during our visits. He constantly cited that we were young and may change our minds in the future. He also reminded us that tragedy could happen where we may lose a child and, as he explained it, a woman would always want a replacement. He recalled an incident with one of his patients that substantiated his point. However, we were determined to keep our family at four. I would live to regret my decision.

November in the Bahamas is weather paradise. The temperature hovers around seventy-five degrees with a soft delicate sea breeze. It's ideal for the outdoors and makes for a comforting time in the islands after the summer heat. After work, Kim and I headed home for an uneventful afternoon. It was not to be.

Shortly after we got home, Kim relieved our Jamaican maid.

"Miss Sands, I done feed the baybe and done burp her too. She was a good baybe today."

With those few words, she was off to the bus stop. Kim went into the kitchen to prepare dinner and shortly afterward went to check on our newborn.

The shrieking cry of my wife made me run to the bedroom.

"Lambert, the baby is not breathing!"

I went into fix-it mode.

"Kim, calm down. Let me see what I can do!"

Kimille's lifeless little body, arms dangling, made me want to cry but I had enough reserve fortitude to at least try CPR. When the ambulance arrived, we continued to try CPR on the way to the hospital to no avail.

At the hospital, the doctors tried without success to revive Kimille. She was gone...gone never to return. The pain that Kim and I endured over the next several weeks was unbearable. We both grieved in different ways. She wanted to share her grief by talking about it with me and others. I climbed into a spiritual hole just wanting the grief to go away.

It was only God's grace and mercy that pulled us through. One afternoon after work, we headed for the beach. The confrontation that we had wasn't easy but it eventually broke down the walls between us. Then the

Lord stepped in and healed our hearts and our marriage. Shortly afterward, God birthed the Marriage Mechanics Ministries. To Him, we owe all the glory and praise!!

If we had prayed before we made our decision, I believe the outcome would have been different. My passivity opened the door for the enemy to bring bad advice. As a result, we reaped the results of our misguided decision. We must remember that when a man neglects or is ignorant of his leadership role, he leaves a void in his home.

In the spirit world, there are no vacuums. There is only God or the devil, good or evil. When a man is passive, it is usually the sign of a deeper spiritual problem. The enemy has a foothold in his life. *The man has not acknowledged his position of authority* and has allowed the enemy to sidetrack him with the spirits of slothfulness, fear and stubbornness. *These are all negative forms of pride: an unwillingness to confront problems and work through them.*

Positive pride is the false motivation that men feel when they are chasing the rainbow of success. Money, promotion and recognition take the place of a viable relationship with the Lord. Negative pride is the slothfulness and lethargy that men feel when they pamper themselves in fear or wallow in depression and inactivity. They avoid problems because they feel powerless and incapable. Eventually, the spirit of procrastination brings failure, debt and unnecessary burdens to the household. This leaves the wife frustrated, and in most cases anxious to assume leadership responsibility.

Modern males growing up without a father figure in their lives are finding it more and more difficult to steer the head of the home position. Some are finding it difficult to provide adequately. Others are unsure which responsibilities are theirs and which are their wives'. The result is a passive, uninformed man whose leadership is vulnerable to resistance and lack. His laid-back attitude gives the devil a loophole to covertly operate a strategy of spoiling the vine with the little foxes.

Economic hardship is one of Satan's most used and effective strategies to reverse biblical order in the home. Unable to provide adequately, a man is pressured to give up the reins of leadership. When Satan attacked Job's livelihood and brought financial ruin, Job's wife told him to curse God and die. He resisted, patiently waited on God, and was blessed more at the end than in the beginning.

Understanding God's plan for dominion and prosperity is the only way to resist Satan's economic strategy of financial lack, instability and reversal of leadership. God has a plan. If we follow His plan and seek His will, He promises to take care of the affairs of our life. Of course, actually *trusting* that promise is up to you.

SO, WHAT IS PROSPERITY?

We are living in a time where people are being taught that having lots of money is prosperity. Using the scripture, *"Beloved, I wish above all things that thou mayest prosper and be in health, even as thy soul prospereth."* *(John 1:2),* the doctrine of prosperity has been preached with fervor. This Satanic deception has produced oppressive, insensitive, and prideful Christians. And in many of these circles, poor people are being trampled upon and neglected. Those who are less fortunate are frowned upon as being ignorant and not having any faith.

The truth behind this erroneous teaching is that money usually showcases the deeper spiritual problems that people have in their lives. Whether by financial abundance or lack thereof, money reveals the pride, insecurity, fear, envy, manipulation, pleasure seeking, and jealousy in people's lives. Money to those who do not operate in dominion is seen as security. And when there is plenty or a little, when it comes or doesn't come, it produces strife, confusion, or depression. The flesh floats right to the top. *"For the love of money is the root of all evil; which while some coveted after, thy have erred from the faith, and pierced themselves through with many sorrows." (Timothy 6:16)*

Money always gives a false sense of security and prosperity. Hence, there are those who seek security in a large bank account and investments.

But Wall Street can crash overnight. Banks can become insolvent. Money should never be put on a pedestal and worshipped because it is only an instrument of commerce. It is an exchange item to be used for goods and services. That's all money is! It should never become an end in itself. Or worse yet, an idol. When money is inordinately sought after, it produces covetousness. Covetousness is a greedy and materialistic mindset that grades people by how much they have. This is the mindset that Jesus told people to avoid at all costs. *"Take heed and beware of covetousness: for a man's life consisteth not in the abundance of the things which he posesseth."* *(Luke 12:15)*

In the Bible, there were many men of God who were affluent. Abraham, Isaac, Job, and Solomon are a few among many who enjoyed God's financial blessing. But note carefully, they did not go after money. God brought the money to them. They obeyed God first, then, God in turn gave them wealth. He was the one that gave the wisdom and knowledge to get the money. *"For the Lord giveth riches and added no sorrow."* The Bible teaches plainly that when riches increase one should never set his heart upon it. Men should always use their gifts and talents to get wealth, but wealth should never replace their love for God. Believing that prosperity means an abundance of physical things is a deception. The Bible says, *"But godliness with contentment is great gain. For we brought nothing into this world and it is certain we can carry nothing out. And having food and raiment let us be therewith content."* *1 Timothy 6:6-8*

True prosperity goes beyond investments in the stock market and a home in a prestigious neighborhood; although it may also include this. The essence of true prosperity is contentment. Am I preaching mediocrity? Of course not! Prosperity means that we are walking in complete wholeness in body, soul and spirit. This comes from an intimate relationship with the Creator rather than merely following a few biblical principles and living in a well-to-do neighborhood.

Prosperity to a Third World person may be an apartment with adequate space and drinking water nearby. In New York City, prosperity may be a spacious high-rise apartment in an upscale neighborhood, in Florida a split-level home on an acre with horses. However, in each case it's not the amount of wealth, rather the satisfaction and pleasure in what one has. This is how prosperity must be viewed. The person who is constantly striving for more and more material things is missing the point if they are seeking fulfillment in things. The creature comforts can never give perfect joy and peace, only the Creator can.

We must all seek God's will for our lives and determine His direction for us. He will give us power to get wealth. God has promised faithfully that if we seek His face, He will add the earthly things that we need to us. God wants His people to be prosperous, and prosperity is being contented with God's blessing upon us: whether in little or in much, our faith and obedience to Him remains unchanged. This is true prosperity and dominion.

GOD'S PLAN FOR FINANCIAL PROSPERITY

"BUT THOU SHALL REMEMBERETH THE LORD THY GOD; FOR IT IS HE THAT GIVETH THEE POWER TO GET WEALTH, THAT HE MAY ESTABLISH HIS COVENANT WHICH HE SWARE UNTO THY FATHERS, AS IT IS THIS DAY." DEUTERONOMY (8:18)

"HONOR THE LORD WITH THY SUBSTANCE, AND WITH THE FIRST FRUITS OF ALL THINE INCREASE: SO SHALL THY BARNS BE FILLED WITH PLENTY, AND THY PRESSES SHALL BURST OUT WITH NEW WINE." (PROVERBS 2:9-10)

"WILL A MAN ROB GOD? YET YE HAVE ROBBED ME. BUT YE SAY, WHEREIN HAVE WE ROBBED THEE? IN TITHES AND OFFERINGS. YE ARE CURSED WITH A CURSE; FOR YE HAVE ROBBED ME, EVEN THIS WHOLE NATION. BRING YE ALL THE TITHES INTO THE STOREHOUSE, THAT THERE MAY BE MEAT IN MINE HOUSE, AND PROVE ME NOW HEREWITH, SAITH THE LORD OF HOST, IF I WILL NOT OPEN YOU THE WINDOWS OF HEAVEN, AND POUR YOU OUT A BLESSING, THAT THERE SHALL NOT BE ROOM ENOUGH TO RECEIVE IT. AND I WILL REBUKE THE DEVOURER FOR YOUR SAKES, AND HE SHALL NOT DESTROY

THE FRUITS OF YOUR GROUND; NEITHER SHALL OUR VINE CAST HER FRUIT BEFORE THE TIME IN THE FIELD, SAITH THE LORD OF HOST. AND ALL NATIONS SHALL CALL YOU BLESSED; FOR YE SHALL BE A DELIGHTSOME LAND, SAITH THE LORD OF HOST." (MALACHI 3:8-12)

"BUT THIS I SAY, HE WHICH SOWETH SPARINGLY SHALL REAP ALSO SPARINGLY; AND HE WHICH SOWETH BOUNTIFULLY SHALL REAP ALSO BOUNTIFULLY. EVERY MAN ACCORDING AS HE PURPOSETH IN HIS HEART, SO LET HIM GIVE; NOT GRUDGINGLY, OR OF NECESSITY; FOR GOD LOVETH A CHEERFUL GIVER." (2 CORINTHIANS 9:6-7)

"GIVE AND IT SHALL BE GIVEN UNTO YOU GOOD MEASURE, PRESS DOWN AND SHAKEN TOGETHER AND RUNNING OVER SHALL MEN GIVE UNTO THY BOSOM. FOR WITH THE SAME MEASURE THAT YE METE WITHAL IT SHALL BE MEASURED TO YOU AGAIN." (LUKE 6:38)

"HE BECOMETH POOR THAT DEALETH WITH A SLACK HAND; BUT THE HAND OF THE DILIGENT MAKETH RICH." (PROVERBS 10:4)

"BE THOU DILIGENT TO KNOW THE STATE OF THY FLOCKS, AND LOOK WELL TO THY HERDS." (PROVERBS 27:24)

"FOR WISDOM IS A DEFENCE, AND MONEY IS A DEFENCE: BUT THE EXCELLENCY OF KNOWLEDGE IS, THAT WISDOM GIVETH LIFE TO THEM THAT HAVE IT." (ECCLESIASTES 7:12)

"MUCH FOOD IS IN THE TILLAGE OF THE POOR; BUT THERE IS THAT IS DESTROYED FOR WANT OF JUDGMENT." (PROVERBS 14:23)

"HE THAT LOVETH PLEASURE SHALL BE A POOR MAN: HE THAT LOVETH WINE AND OIL SHALL NOT BE RICH." (PROVERBS 21:17)

"HE ALSO THAT IS SLOTHFUL IN HIS WORK IS BROTHER TO HIM THAT IS A GREAT WASTER." (PROVERBS 18:9)

As long as we are upon this earth, we must remember that money is our means of upkeep. The wise man Solomon puts it this way, *"A feast is made for laughter, and wine maketh merry: but **money answereth all things**." (Ecclesiastes 10:19)* So, when God puts money in our hand, we need to know what to do. If we don't pay attention and be alert, the enemy sends the little foxes that ruin the vine. In other words, always be vigilant with your resources. Herein lies the way to prosperity, contentment, and dominion.

Firstly, when God gives money He expects us to honor and recognize the Person who gave it. This is called tithing and giving. We should take a tenth of our income and deposit it in the house of God, along with other monetary gifts. Then we must pay those we owe for services and goods we have purchased: light, water, telephone, groceries, etc. Then, we should consider those who are in need. Then comes savings, investment and pleasure!

Giving is a fundamental teaching of the kingdom of God that we can never circumvent. It is a sign of love and self-sacrifice when it is done out of obedience and compassion. When a person is operating in dominion they can give their last and still feel good. They can give to those in need and not think they were "had." Money is not the issue, God's will is. When we are shackled by our fleshly thinking, we are always looking out for number one. We are overly concerned about our own needs. Wisdom and faith gives us the freedom and confidence to look beyond the few dollars that we give to God who is able to supply all our needs.

When we give we can expect God to give back to us, according to His word. It may not come the day after we have put fifty dollars in the offering or after our tithes envelope was collected, but it will come. God's timing is different from ours. While we are looking through imperfect faith and a dark glass, God in His sovereignty knows exactly when to let the blessing flow. Many people become frustrated when God doesn't show up when they expect Him. However, I am learning to relax, let go, and let God. Prosperity will come!

While operating in faith, we must always be open to the voice of God and be flexible when He wants us to change the routine a little. For example, I had just taken my tithe money from my bank account to carry to church on Sunday. I was walking out to lunch, when I met a Christian brother who I had not seen for almost a year. The Holy Spirit said, "Give him fifty dollars." Being open to the voice of God, I obeyed and gave my brother the fifty dollars as the Spirit had instructed me to do. Some people would have immediately started rebuking the devil. But what was more important, a brother in desperate need, or carrying the tithe to church on Sunday? Yes, God wants us to be obedient in our tithing but I am sure He is much more concerned about the brother in desperate need. One need was more urgent that the other. This is faith and dominion; flowing in the Spirit of God! A year later, that same brother related to me how God had really met his need that day.

But while we operate in faith and dominion we must guard against passivity. When a man exhibits passivity in financial management, the Devil can wreak havoc on a marriage and family. Many marriages have been dissolved because of poor financial management and debt burden. With proper financial management in place the family can be spared much anguish, frustration and embarrassment. Also, when a man exercises sound financial management, it shows good leadership skills that will gain the respect of his wife.

But who should handle the money? How much money should be spent without advising your spouse? What about debt servicing and purchasing of assets? Time and time again, I hear men say that they are not proficient in the area of financial management or some other area and have turned this duty over to their wives. Whereas, a man should welcome his wife's advice, talents and assistance, he cannot give up the responsibility of overseer and leader. If he does, it's a sure sign of slothfulness and ignorance in leadership. Remember, a good leader never does all the work and must delegate tasks to others. So, if your wife is proficient in finances, you are a blessed man, let her help you. Give her the opportunity to budget in consultation with you; however, continue to be alert and watchful as a good steward over the blessing that God has given you.

Sit down with your wife to discuss and come to agreement with regard to spending of the family's income. This is the sign of a good leader who recognizes that he cannot do it alone. The husband and the wife are designed to operate as one unit. Listen to your wife's advice and implement those things you know will benefit the family. This will serve to eliminate strife and insecurity that sometimes arise, when one spouse is unaware of what the other spouse is doing with the money.

When you have done this, learn to dominate money, this is the key to financial prosperity. Never allow money to dominate you! Develop habits of budgeting and thriftiness. Develop habits of maximizing income and minimizing expenses. Listen to the Spirit of God as He gives wisdom and direction while shopping or spending. Pay attention to household expenses to ensure conservation and prudence.

Try to conserve as much as possible, but don't be a prig or slave driver about it. Being critical and overbearing will ostracize your family. Rather, use the gentle but firm approach coupled with love. If you are in your spiritual position, the Holy Spirit will help motivate family members. Just do your part of encouragement to conserve.

A good way to conserve is by learning to do some repairs and maintenance work yourself. God can give you wisdom to be a handyman! This can cut down enormously on the household budget. For example, the house needs painting or the car may need a tune-up. Don't wait until the walls of your home become an eyesore, or the car stalls on a major highway, before you react. Be proactive instead of reactionary, look for wear and tear and fix and maintain as needed. The Bible says, that the way of the slothful is as a hedge of thorns but the way of the just is plain. In this scripture, laziness is polarized with being righteous. Laziness is rebellion against God's firm mandate for fervency in business.

FREEDOM FROM SELF – THE WAY TO EXCELLENCE

."THE SLUGGARD IS WISER IN HIS OWN CONCEIT THAN SEVEN MEN THAT CAN RENDER A REASON." (PROVERBS 26:16)

"HE ALSO THAT IS SLOTHFUL IN HIS WORK IS BROTHER TO HIM
THAT IS A GREAT WASTER." (PROVERBS 18:9)

So long as we are in love with ourselves, we will never let go and let God. He wants so much to endow us with supernatural wisdom and energize us with His power, so that we could confront challenges instead of running from them. The Lord wants to flow through us like a river, but we cling to the old wineskin and old garments instead of letting go and letting God. Divine wisdom is available for all men. All we have to do is ask, *"If any of you lack wisdom, let him ask of God, that giveth to all men liberally, and upbraideth not; and it shall be given him. But let him ask in faith nothing wavering. For he that wavereth is like a wave of the sea driven with the wind and tossed." (James 1:5-6)*

Usually when we see lethargy in men, we assume that it is a discipline problem. In a superficial way, lack of discipline may have played a part in this behavior. However, behind this slothfulness lies a spirit of negative pride. Lethargy is born from a stubborn and fearful spirit that avoids problems and work instead of accepting and working through challenges. The cure for negative pride is not the school of discipline as most think. The school of discipline may help, but it will still leave the cancer of negative pride intact. Pride has to be broken through humility and genuine repentance. This is God's way to bring a man to a higher level of discipline where he can confront challenges and work through them.

I think if anyone has struggled with faith and dominion, it's me. It seemed that every time I came that close to defeating debt and bringing prosperity to my family, the enemy would step in and create havoc financially. Then instead of listening to my wife's tender rebuke and advice, I would continue the endless cycle of borrowing. I just had to do it just one more time. Ah! If I could just do it over again! But God knows all things and these experiences can benefit a man who is determined not to walk the halls of mediocrity, when everything is available to him.

My problem was not that I spent too much or was pleasure centered, although some of that may have contributed to my dilemma. My problem was patience. Patience to sit back, relax, and enjoy the ride. I simply refused to let God take the lead. My opinion, my fears, and insecurity usually drowned out the voice of God, making me susceptible to Satan's lies. Like an adulterous woman, I was making love to two men. I wanted God to lead, I prayed that He would lead me but I always depended on my own human reasoning.

But our God wants us to move forward in pure and absolute faith. This means listening only to His voice. Yes, he wants our debts repaid, our family in order and our children saved. But we retreat too often in fear and insecurity. I am here to encourage you, man of God, that you are more than a conqueror. The victory has already been won. All God wants you to do is distribute the spoils. The Devil constantly puts up mirages before us. "It's not going to work out. You'll be a fool to listen to that. People have been trying that faith business for years and they haven't succeeded." Don't listen to him! Faith is your victory!!! God is our Father and He will never let us down. The Bible says to us that we should let God be true and every man a liar and God has said, *"Behold, I give unto you power to tread on serpents and scorpions, and over all the power of the enemy and nothing shall by any means hurt you." (Luke 10:10)*

DEFENDING MY AUTHORITY

INTRODUCTION

One of the most miraculous and astounding stories in the Bible describes a man of God named Elijah performing a mind boggling supernatural act. Under clear skies, and surrounded by a multitude of people, Elijah called down fire from heaven! Man, oh man! No one in history, except Moses, had ever been used by God to do something like that. But guess what? One day later Elijah was high-tailing out of Jerusalem, running from a woman.

True story! But, why would a man of such power and authority suddenly turn and run fearing for his life? The answer: Jezebel, a woman who controlled and manipulated authority in the city of Jerusalem. She had enough spiritual and political clout to cause the man of God to run. Wow!

Disillusioned, full of self-pity and insecurity, Elijah ran into the wilderness wanting just to find a place where he could die. His plight and his eventual turn-about is a spiritual lesson that every man must learn...*and learn it quickly!* There is an all-out war to emasculate men and corrupt authority in the household and every male is in danger!

We are living in the final stages of the last days and it has come down to this: fight or die! Stand up or shut up! The enemy is all around us and closing in fast for the kill. We must resist him at all cost. You are under attack! Satan has sent Jezebel, Delilah and Anger; his three most powerful anti-male spirits to frustrate and destroy you.

Fearing confrontation and the dark wisdom of Jezebel, most men have dug in deep into their foxholes. They have compromised their authority for appeasement. *"Let's not rock the boat,"* they say. Others, deceived and subdued by Delilah's sexual prowess are content to abandon the home to fulfill their sexual appetites. Then, there are those who are full of bitterness and anger and have become dominant and abusive.

My prayer is that your mind and heart would be open to what is oppressing you and how to gain victory. Satan wants you out of the way so that he can denominate the family and destroy the home. Without Godly authority in the home, our children will become corrupt and the <u>earth will be judged.</u> He knows this, and is working overtime to bring this about. But here is the good news: you can stop the tide of ungodliness in your home and any place that you bear authority. It must begin with you regaining authority…one step at a time!

CHAPTER 4

THE DEADLY SPIRIT OF JEZEBEL

The first time Daron saw Jasmin, she was ministering at a youth out-reach rally. He was impressed; she appeared to be an angel from heaven. Coupled with her attractiveness, the gifts of the Holy Spirit seemed to flow from her like a river. She told people their whole life story. She preached with an unusual authority and with such forcefulness that even the pastor of the rally cringed in his seat. The crowds flocked to hear this young evangelist expound the word of God. There were many testimonies of deliverance and healing.

From that moment, Daron wanted to marry Jasmin. He was a successful businessman and had been single for a number of years. He wanted a wife and this young woman, he thought, would make a great wife. After the revival was over, Daron got in touch with Jasmin and they quickly began a courtship. Within months they were married.

But what the unsuspecting Daron did not know was that he was signing his spiritual death warrant when he decided to tie the knot with Jasmin. The first few months of the marriage seemed to be 'a dream come true' for Daron. He had managed to get a Christian wife that had 'the total package.' His evangelist wife was always on call to preach services and run revivals and he got recognition along with her. But, the fantasy soon came to an end as Daron came to grips with reality. As time went on, and the children came, Jasmin seemed not to realize that her ministry also included her husband and her children. Numerous weekends would find Jasmin on missions leaving Daron to be the househusband.

Daron told Jasmin that they should spend a little more time together, especially since their family had grown. He told her that he felt that they were spending a considerable amount of time in church services without paying attention to family duties. But instead of getting a listening ear of submission from his evangelist wife, he got a sharp rebuke! Jasmin gave him an earful about how carnal and immature he was.

Of course, this was a rude awakening for Daron, but it did not end there. This became the catalyst that started the ball of religious insanity bouncing in his house. Jasmin seemed bent on letting him know who should be in charge of the home. As far as she was concerned, she was the more spiritual one and that qualified her to make the final decisions in the house. Daron was pushed aside like a little puppy by the big dog that was now ready for her food. She treated him with utter contempt. Even in front of people, she would let it be known that she called the shots and Daron was merely a figurehead.

Between her mother and church, Jasmin was never home long enough to cook a proper meal or even clean house. She was always on the go. Revival and outreach were top on her list. "She was doing the work of God," she had told Daron. The bewildered husband felt betrayed and confused, he thought he had done the right thing by choosing this spiritual woman for his wife. But now, the angel had suddenly turned into a demon! He felt alone and abandoned. Depression began to set in. He even started to wonder if this was what Christianity was all about.

Even in the bedroom he felt the brunt of Jasmin's pigheadedness. She would go on long fasts without asking her husband's permission -- then rebuke him for wanting too much sex. The pressure got to the point that he felt that he needed to find relief and release. He felt that he was going out of his mind, and each day, the temptation to find satisfaction with another woman grew stronger and stronger.

Poor Daron, he made a deadly oversight when he picked Jasmin, looking for a religious woman instead of a Godly one, but alas, it was too late to turn back the wheels of time. When people saw them together, it appeared as though they had a great marriage. The sermons were great, they both smiled and grinned on the outside but inside they were both dying. The spirit of Jezebel now smothered and overshadowed Daron's manhood. After ten years of marriage, he moved out and divorced Jasmin to the shock and dismay of the church community. The game playing was over!

* * *

DISCERNING AND UNDERSTANDING THE JEZEBEL SPIRIT

The two most deadly spirits sent by Satan to destroy men are Jezebel and Delilah. These names are taken from two women in the Bible who used their feminine wiles and influence to manipulate and control men. When these spirits are embodied by the feminine gender, their aim is to hinder, frustrate and prevent men from operating in Godly authority. However, by far, the deadlier of the two is the spirit of Jezebel. The above story illustrates how frustrating and debilitating a woman who is bent on "ruling her man" can be. The Bible in two of its wisdom books point to this.

> "And I find more bitter than death the woman, whose heart is snares and nets, and her hands as bands: whoso pleaseth God shall escape from her; but the sinner shall be taken by her." (Ecclesiastes 7:26)

> "A virtuous woman is a crown to her husband: but she that maketh ashamed is as rottenness in his bones." (Proverbs 12:4)

> "It is better to dwell in the corner of the housetop, than with a brawling woman and in a wide house." (Proverbs 25:24)

The Spirit of Jezebel chokes and clogs up a man's divine supply, leaving him to wallow in emasculation and impotence. He is powerless in his own home and eventually gives up authority to appease his wife. **The image of God**, of a female submitting to a male, and masculinity covering femininity, is corrupted. The children of this relationship become insecure and are easy prey for the lesbian, transgender, bisexual and homosexual spirit. They also have the seeds of domination and control sowed into their hearts, and they carry these spirits into their relationships.

Unlike any other spirit, this deadly spirit destroys a man from within. Instead of providing help, encouragement and compassion, her constant aim is to seize control. By hindering, frustrating, conniving and total defiance against his leadership, she wears him down. Feeling isolated, he gives in or gives up the reins of leadership. At that point, the devil can consolidate his position in the home by producing unrighteous seed (spiritually wounded children) and use the wife to do further damage in her church and community by releasing this ungodly spirit wherever she goes.

The Jezebel spirit is now rampant in the Western world as false equality is being heralded as the modern truth. There is a massive media campaign of indoctrination. Words like "sexist" and "misogynist" are now used as intimidation. People and women in particular, are being taught to abandon the age-old proven roles of men and women and adopt a more neutral, liberal, and "fair" attitude of equality. Subtly, they are being taught that there is really no difference between the genders. In truth, however, this is just a clandestine effort by Satan and his cohorts to undermine authority in the home and reduce the male role to simply being a dummy (pardon the pun). Whereas men and women are equal, God is a God of order, and as a masterful and perfect designer of masculinity and femininity, He wants them to embrace His word and roles for their lives.

WHERE DID THE JEZEBEL SPIRIT COME FROM?

When the name Jezebel is mentioned, most people associate it with make-up, jewelry or excessive outward adornment in some form. And although this spirit may encompass this outward adornment, few people understand the depth of who Jezebel really was. Jezebel was the daughter of King Ethbaal, king of the Zidonians, an ungodly pagan nation that were the enemies of Israel. This lady became influential in the governing of Israel through her marriage to Ahab who became King of Israel after the death of his father, Omri, a very ungodly man. After Jezebel became the wife of Ahab, the nation fell into its lowest state of morality since its beginning.

> "AND AHAB THE SON OF OMRI DID EVIL IN THE SIGHT OF THE LORD ABOVE ALL THAT WERE BEFORE HIM. AND IT CAME TO PASS, AS IF IT HAD BEEN A LIGHT THING FOR HIM TO WALK IN THE SINS OF JEROBOAM THE SON NEBAT, THAT HE TOOK TO WIFE JEZEBEL THE DAUGHTER OF ETHBAAL KING OF THE ZIDONIANS, AND WENT AND SERVED BAAL AND WORSHIPPED HIM. AND HE REARED UP AN ALTAR FOR BAAL IN THE HOUSE OF BAAL, WHICH HE HAD BUILT IN SAMARIA. AND AHAB MADE A GROVE, AND <u>AHAB DID MORE TO PROVOKE THE LORD GOD OF ISRAEL TO ANGER THAN ALL THE KINGS OF ISRAEL THAT WERE BEFORE HIM</u>." (1 KINGS 16:30-33)

Behind this woman, Jezebel, was a **deadly domineering** and **religious** spirit that she brought with her to the nation of Israel; a spirit that rearranged the teaching and holiness of God's people. One of the first things that she did was to kill and persecute the true prophets of God. After this, she proceeded to flood the land with false teaching from her own ungodly and pagan nation. Her husband was King, but he only carried the title. Jezebel "ruled things" and her ungodly control saturated a once Godly nation. Subtly and persistently, she exercised control concealed by the King's throne. This is one of the main reasons that this spirit is so effective. By operating *from behind* a concealed position: her husband, her pastor, a worldwide ministry, she can do immense damage without being in the forefront.

Have you ever talked to a man and discovered that he did not have a mind of his own? He was seemingly oblivious to making any decision or directing his own life? Or he had no power to direct his family; a man who was afraid to be the leader of his home because of the domineering spirit of his wife? Today, because of social and economic changes in society and rebellion against God's word, the spirit of Jezebel has entered most homes turning them spiritually upside down. The husband has been dispossessed from his headship or leadership role because of ignorance and spiritual powerlessness.

Some women claim that they have to take over the running of the home because of the lackadaisical and passive attitude of their husbands. In other cases, a misguided husband relinquishes authority feeling insecure and inadequate beside his brilliant, educated and capable wife. However, I say this without compromise; any man who gives up the leadership of his home to his wife will reap the bitter results of his ignorance or inept decisions. God will not bless disobedience or rejection of His word. No doubt, there may be cases where a woman has to take over leadership in the home because the husband may be sick, injured or absent. But in the normal circumstances, whether a woman is more intelligent, frugal, sensible, spiritual or aggressive, God's model for the family should always be maintained.

For some men who have subscribed to the feminist movement or modern rationale of equality, this biblical model sounds unfair and backward. But remember, "the God factor" is what most people leave out of their thinking and marriage. Even if a husband is not as smart, frugal or aggressive as his wife, this does not change his position in the home. **This does not mean he should foolishly run his home without the assistance of his capable wife.** However, he should never give up the reins that God has placed in his hands. He should submit himself to God and allow the Holy Spirit to give him wisdom and understanding in directing his home. *"If any man lack wisdom let him ask of God who giveth to all men liberally and abraideth not. And it shall be given him. But let him ask in faith nothing wavering for he that wavereth is like a wave driven by the sea and tossed."* (James 1:5-6)

Men during the past century have become susceptible to entrapment by the spirit of Jezebel <u>because of their own lack of dedication, faith in God,</u>

<u>and selflessness.</u> The Spirit of Jezebel appeals to a man's hidden desires and ambitions. A bigger house, a better car, influence and respect in the community became more important than integrity and godliness. It feeds on the pride, fear and insecurities in a man's life. This is the spirit that offers excellent ideas to succeed at one's selfish ambitions contrary to God's will. A perfect example of this can be found in 1 Kings 21. Ahab wanted to expand his royal property, but in order to do this, he needed to purchase an adjacent piece of property belonging to a man by the name of Naboth.

When Ahab asked Naboth to purchase his vineyard, he was turned down flat! He was upset and threw a pity party. Jezebel, after seeing her whining husband, decided that she would get the field for him. She secretly wrote a letter to the elders of Israel advising them to proclaim a public fast, and allow Naboth to sit in a prominent place during the fast. After the fast was over, she instructed them to have two ungodly men accuse Naboth, claiming that he had blasphemed God. Then the elders were to condemn him and have him stoned.

Jezebel's plans succeeded, and Naboth was stoned to death by the inhabitants. But, who was the real culprit? Who really allowed it to happen? Ahab. It was his secret desire. He was deceived by his own lustful desire for material gain. The spirit of Jezebel needs a weak, two-faced, and insecure man like Ahab to operate. Many times, when we see a woman who is dominating her husband, we assume that he needs to be stronger and "force" her into submission.

However, the reality is, without Ahab, Jezebel is weakened. The spirit of Jezebel is feeding off the pride, stubbornness, disobedience and insecurities that hide under his hypocritical, passive and so-called "humble" demeanor. When the devil comes, he is always looking for something that he deposited. This is the same spirit that attacked Jesus in the wilderness. "Showcase your divine power, get the people to worship you, seek your own fame and feed your selfish desires." This was Satan's word to Jesus. But he could find nothing in the Son of God. Jesus was pure, holy and _**full of humility**_. Satan was knocked down every time he tried to defeat Jesus.

This reminds me of a Pastor who took over a new church. Almost instantly, changes in the ministry were made without regard for senior staff. Their positions were made redundant. At first, nobody knew why these drastic changes were being made. Not long after, the church secretary who had been employed by the church for many years was dismissed; that's when the truth finally surfaced. Then, it became obvious who was behind the changes and who really ran things. Behind the scenes, this Pastor's wife ran the show and anyone who crossed her was cut down without reservation. This is a classic case of the Jezebel spirit.

Another unique aspect of the spirit of Jezebel is its uncanny ability to mimic the prophetic and wisdom gifts of the spirit of God. *Remember, Jezebel had four hundred prophets at her disposal; four hundred lying prophets!* Her aim was to inundate the land of Israel with ***false light or false prophecy***. In other words: witchcraft! Prophecy that appeals to your flesh and things that you want. Or, prophecy that circumvents the true move of God. Prophecy and false light that appeals to insecurity, pride and fear.

Have you ever wondered how a person could have so much word of God or prophecy, yet miss out on, "Love thy neighbor as thyself." Or how can someone be prophesying and slandering the pastor at the same time. Or, have so much prophetic insight yet be rebellious, disobedient and not know how to treat her own husband? *"Ye shall know them by their fruits. Do men gather grapes of thorns, or figs of thistles?"* (Matthew 7:16) *"He that saith he is in the light, and hateth his brother, is in darkness even until now."* (1 John 2: 9)

DEFEATING JEZEBEL

As the leader in the home, you must resist and cast this ungodly spirit out of your marriage. **The key to doing this is by taking the higher ground spiritually.** If this spirit is in your household, it may be feeding off something in your nature. Scripture clearly indicates that Satan has a legal right to dominate prideful and arrogant people. Job 41:34 *"He beholdeth all high things: he is a king over all the children of pride."* **You**

<u>must repent and renounce pride and disobedience in your life without</u> <u>delay. Humble yourself before God. Humble yourself!!!</u> Ask God for insight into your character. <u>This is a powerful spirit</u> and will not leave easily. <u>Jesus said that this kind cometh not forth execpt by fasting and prayer. Hasty prayers, lack of consecration, and *male arrogance* will keep you in bondage to Jezebel.</u>

<u>Keen spiritual insight and total selflessness will be your only path to complete victory.</u> Only God can give you spiritual insight to know the difference between **help** and **control**; **advice** and **manipulation**. Adam's mistake was listening to Satan's lie that God was holding back on something that would make him so much better. Satan created in Adam a secret ambition or pride "to desire worship." This led to Adam's spiritual demise. Men will not be successful against the spirit of Jezebel if they have some secret agenda. He must be dead to self and alive to God. When Satan came against Jesus, he found a slate that only had the commandments of God written on it. *"...for the prince of this world cometh, and hath nothing in me."* (John 16:30)

After his great revival service on Mount Carmel, the Prophet Elijah thought that victory over Jezebel was assured and complete. Surely, Jezebel would now see that the God of the Hebrews was the True and Living God and would repent of her wickedness. But to his utter chagrin, Jezebel sent a message to the man of God that his life was in danger, and he was on her hit list. And guess what? The man of miracles, God's man of faith and power, ran for his life! Incredible! Discouraged and heartbroken he sought death. Jezebel found a chord of self-preservation in his life and she played her tune.

"AND AHAB TOLD JEZEBEL ALL THAT ELIJAH HAD DONE AND WITHAL HOW THEY HAD SLAIN ALL THE PROPHETS WITH THE SWORD. THEN JEZEBEL SENT A MESSENGER UNTO ELIJAH SAYING. SO LET THE GODS DO TO ME AND MORE ALSO, IF I MAKE NOT THY LIFE AS THE LIFE OF ONE OF THEM BY TOMORROW ABOUT THIS TIME. AND WHEN HE SAW THAT, HE AROSE, AND WENT FOR HIS LIFE, AND CAME TO BEERSHEBA, WHICH,

BELONGETH TO JUDAH, AND LEFT HIS SERVANT THERE. BUT
HE HIMSELF WENT A DAY'S JOURNEY INTO THE WILDERNESS
AND CAME AND SAT DOWN UNDER A JUNIPER TREE: AND HE
REQUESTED FOR HIMSELF THAT HE MIGHT DIE; AND SAID, IT
IS ENOUGH NOW, O LORD, TAKE AWAY MY LIFE; FOR I AM NOT
BETTER THAN MY FATHERS." (1 KINGS 19:1-4)

The man of God had thrown his best blow, but Jezebel was still standing.
Now he had to regroup. He needed a word from the Lord. But God wanted him to have a deeper and richer understanding of His power. When Elijah came to Mount Horeb, after fasting for forty days, God unveiled to Elijah more of His unfathomable wisdom. God passed by Elijah with a strong wind, an earthquake, and fire. But He revealed Himself to Elijah by a still, small voice. Elijah had moved in the great power of God. He knew God's demonstration in miraculous feats, but there was something more God wanted to get across to Elijah: **relationship**. *It is only when a man has touched the heart of God can Jezebel truly be removed.*

After a great move of God, if you really don't understand the inner working of God's word, you will always fall prey to insecurity and pride. Mountaintop experiences will come and go, feelings come and go, but if we have a genuine relationship with the Master, we learn to weather all storms. **Our security is not in what God does, nor our feelings of righteousness, but in who He is, and understanding His ways.** He made known His ways unto Moses, his acts unto the children of Israel. **Psalm 103:7** What are His ways: love, mercy, righteous judgment, graciousness, humility... *"But the wisdom that is from above is first pure, then peaceable, gentle, and easy to be entreated, full of mercy and good fruits, without partiality, and without hypocrisy..." (James 3:17)*

This deeper realm of quietness and stillness of God's character is not easy to perceive neither easily entered. It can only be entered when pride has been broken in a man's heart: pride about himself. He no longer grades people by their race or gender. He no longer feels superior about himself. He has come to a place of true humility and is completely depending on God. Even people with heavy anointing like Elijah could have missed it.

God was using him greatly, but do you detect pride in his voice when he was making fun of the prophets of Baal, while God was performing the miracle? He had not yet tasted of the unveiled wisdom that comes from the secret quietness of relationship.

This is the wisdom given when we stand still and know that He is God. Our spirits are frozen in awe at His immense glory and power. We cannot move, but must simply listen and obey. Then He can pour Himself into us. If God unveils Himself to you, it means you walk in Light. You know the true nature of things around you. The truth behind events, situations and the human spirit is also unveiled to you. *"For every one that useth milk is unskillful in the word of righteousness: for he is a babe. But strong meat belongeth to them that are of full age, even those who by reason of use have their senses exercised to discern both good and evil."* (Hebrews 5:13-14)

With this wisdom you can easily defeat Jezebel because you stand upon the higher ground. When Elijah returned from the mountain, he knew without a shadow of doubt that Jezebel would be eaten up by dogs like God said. His flesh was dead, and his spirit man was now soaring in the light of God's word and his elevated relationship with the Father. **He feared only God!!!**

Many times, in my own marriage, my wife reached for the leadership reins during times when I appeared weak or made errors. But, being focused and submitting myself to God always kept our marriage on the right path. I refused to give up my authority because of the inner voice that said, *"That's not the right way."* Indeed, I did make mistakes that caused family debt and hardship, but the way out was not reversal of the marriage relationship. The way out was a deeper relationship with God where I could hear His voice clearly and obey Him when He spoke.

Do not falter or give up when your wife demeans or disrespects you. The Jezebel spirit will cause a woman to be vicious and extremely treacherous, especially when she doesn't get her own way. She may withdraw sexually or try to ruin your reputation when you do not obey her wishes. Nonetheless, remain committed and faithful to your marriage but do not compromise your leadership. Men who try to appease their wives will find out that appeasement does not work. The Allies during World War Two tried to appease Hitler by allowing him to continually annex various countries under German control. But this only fueled Hitler's lust for more and more power. It was only when they took a concerted stand that they were able to stop this aggressive dictator.

In fact, the greatest threat to manhood in our century is the Jezebel spirit. Jezebel is responsible for the gender insecurities that children now feel as daddy gives up the authority in the home. With no leadership and no direction, children are succumbing to the lesbian, homosexual, bisexual and transgender spirits that destroy morality and produce a reprobate mind that hates the idea of God.

You must take a stand! However, if your wife proceeds with her defiance of your authority and leadership, don't turn to the flesh. It will be a big mistake. Abuse and strife will not solve your problem, they will only heighten them. Your wife's submission must be given willing. Like Jesus, use the word to educate and encourage your wife but do not try to "beat her down" with the word. Be firm and calm. You are the victor because Satan was defeated at Calvary.

Love is still the most powerful overcoming power. Even as your wife continues her rebellious behavior, react in love. This does not mean that you should give in to her every desire. But love her despite the constant rebellious attitude that she displays. The deadly Jezebel spirit has attacked all women in their marriages at some time or the other. Many are ignorant that it festers in their lives.

Your wife may have grown up in a home where her mother was dominant or the father may have been abusive. She has grown up in a society that has accepted the feminist ideology in some form or the other. She may have suffered from incest, or betrayal of trust. Her hurts and insecurities have opened her heart to this spirit. It will take time to heal. Patiently, gently and lovingly lead her to Christ and the healing power available at Calvary.

The battle will become ferocious as you block Satan's plan. He will fight you tooth and nail, to get you to retreat. But don't despair. The woman of God is too precious to lose to the spirit of Jezebel. She is your ticket to another dimension of marital life. Hold on, God is with you and will not let you down. The results may not come overnight. But you will reap, if you faint not!

CHAPTER 5

WHY, WHY, WHY...OH DELILAH!

Rick stared in disbelief. The house looked as if thieves had ransacked it. All the furniture was gone; the refrigerator was empty; the kitchen cupboard doors were open with just a few cans of soup still inside. But that gnawing feeling inside his stomach told him that this was not the work of intruders. The heated argument that he'd had with Karen earlier that day only fueled his assumptions. Karen had left him!

Karen had made it clear to Rick that she would not tolerate his adulterous lifestyle anymore. She had stomached enough. Fear of AIDS had added to her stress and anxiety bringing her to the brink of a nervous breakdown. Even after pleading with him, he continued stubbornly in his adulterous ways. It seemed as if an unseen force drove him and he was somehow ignorant of the pain and suffering that he was inflicting upon his family, and the woman he once loved and romanced.

Karen was a soft-spoken, homely girl who rarely argued unless seriously provoked. She was not ostentatious and very frugal when it came to money. Although she was not a Christian, her strong Christian parental roots impacted her lifestyle and she remained a virgin until marriage. Karen's fairytale childhood dream was to have a happy marriage with children. But to her utter disillusionment, her husband, Rickford Shanley, became a never-ending nightmare.

She had met Rick on a double date while in high school. He was ruggedly handsome and very romantic. They "hit it off" almost immediately, and began going steady. Karen heard that a lot of girls were attracted to Rick, but she was undaunted. She believed that her love for him would overshadow any feminine opposition. After high school, they attended the same college. There, they continued the steady relationship but again the nagging rumors surfaced about Rick having other relationships. After college, they quickly tied the knot, but Karen would live to regret her decision.

Only four months after the marriage, Karen began receiving calls from a mysterious person who quickly hung up when she answered the phone. Coupled with this, her suspicions were heightened when she found an unsigned love letter in the car's glove compartment. Then there were the unaccounted hours of his whereabouts. On several occasions, she found nude pictures of women sprawled across his social media page on the internet. But even then, Karen decided to hold on to her childhood dream. She was going to make her marriage work "no matter what."

But her nightmare had just begun. When she approached him about her concerns, he became defensive and violent. Finally, the darts that would pierce her spirit caught up with her. It happened on a Friday afternoon when she had come home early from work. She found Rick in bed with one of his co-workers. For a moment Karen thought that her world had ended, but Rick begged for forgiveness with tears streaming down his face. He told her that it would never happen again, and Karen decided that she would give him another chance. But another chance seemed to be all he wanted. After this incident, she caught him several more times with other women.

After two years of marriage, Karen had had enough. That morning, a young female had called the house demanding to speak to Rick. This, of course, inflamed Karen and they had a bitter argument. When Karen left for work that morning, Rick could see the hurt and pain in her eyes.

Whatever flame was left in the marriage was extinguished. But he never thought she would ever leave.

As Rick stood looking over the empty house, tears came to his eyes. Why, why did he continue to do it he asked himself? He wanted his wife. He wanted his marriage. But how could he change? He had tried to change before but it always failed. Was he doomed to be like this for the rest of his life?

WHERE DID DELILAH COME FROM?

Like Rick, most men's sexual problems start long before they tie the marital knot and long before they are caught in adultery. It is during their early teenage years that Delilah finds a way into their lives. During these years, men are expected to have sexual experiences. It is a part of the macho image of being a real man. It doesn't matter which girl or even if love is involved. The objective is to "chalk-up" as many experiences as you can. This, of course, inflates your male ego or as some would say, "It makes you a man."

The internet, pornographic magazines and elicit sexual relationships are some of the ways men open up their lives to sexual spirits. In time, they are blinded to the fact that Delilah, the sexual perverse spirit has taken up residence in their lives. They appear normal to most people, but these same men eventually destroy their families and marriages because of their inability to control their sexual appetites.

Once it takes root in the male psyche, the spirit of Delilah is difficult to uproot because of its addictive, pervasive and deceptive nature. She promises pleasure but brings much pain. She comforts and tantalizes him with her smooth tongue, but her words are empty and her promises are lies. She is like Alice in Wonderland; she keeps him in her dream world until he is weakened and demoralized. Then, she moves on to greener pastures and other ignorant men.

Delilah represents the power of influence in its fallen state. God gave woman the power of influence to create unity and compatibility in marriage. Her influence comes from her attractive feminine character and love for details. The feminine character embodies the power of submission. It willingly accepts the male as leader and strengthens him. By accepting him as the leader she can influence his decisions. She offers insight and fine details, which he sometimes misses. She is like the fruitful vineyard that multiplies the seeds he plants.

But in its corrupt state, this gift degenerates into fleshly ostentation. She advertises her feminine curves instead of inner character qualities. Her dress code highlights the bust-line, waist and thighs. She uses her words to tantalize and create in him a hunger for more and more sex. Her main aim is to conquer him through his strong sexual drive.

Although the spirit of Delilah may not stop a man initially, it destroys his credibility and causes his leadership to stagnate. He has to lie to cover his tracks. He loses his leadership focus as he expends energy sexually in adulterous relationships. He may be driven by his lust to spend endless hours looking at pornographic material on the internet, on videos, and in magazines. Delilah is the strange woman that the Bible tells us to beware of. *"For the lips of a strange woman drop as a honeycomb, and her mouth is smoother than oil: But her end is bitter as wormwood, sharp as a two-edged sword. Her feet go down to death; her steps take hold on hell. Lest thou shouldest ponder the path of life, her ways are moveable, that thou canst not know them." (Proverbs 5:3-6)* Men who embrace this sexually immoral spirit live to regret they ever allowed it into their lives. The story of Samson illustrates this.

"AND WHEN DELILAH SAW THAT HE HAD TOLD HER ALL HIS HEART, SHE SENT AND CALLED FOR THE LORDS OF THE PHILISTINES, SAYING, COME UP THIS ONE, FOR HE HATH SHEWED ME ALL HIS HEART. THEN THE LORDS OF THE PHILISTINES CAME UP UNTO HER, AND BROUGHT MONEY IN THEIR HAND. AND SHE MADE HIM SLEEP UPON HER KNEES; AND SHE CALLED FOR A MAN, AND SHE CAUSED HIM TO SHAVE OFF THE SEVEN LOCKS OF HIS HEAD; AND SHE BEGAN TO AFFLICT HIM, AND HIS STRENGTH WENT FROM HIM. AND SHE SAID, THE

Philistines be upon thee, Samson. And he awoke out of his sleep, and said, I will go out as at other times before, and shake myself And he wist not that the Lord was departed from him. But the Philistines took him and put out his eyes, and brought him down to Gaza, and bound him with fetters of brass; and he did grind in the prison house." (Judges 16:18-21)

Samson was a man used mightily by God. But his sexual weakness became his undoing. Sex was Samson's Achilles heel and Delilah found it. Now she could control and manipulate him by keeping him in a fantasy world believing that she really loved him. Eventually, she got him to reveal the secret to his strength. After that, Samson found himself in a Philistine jail with his eyes gouged out and attached to a grinding mill. Men who are in bondage to their sexual desires fare no better. Few ever figure out why they divorced their wonderful wives for the nightclub stripper or office slut.

PROTECT YOUR SEXUAL DESIRES

"Flee Fornication, every sin that a man doeth is without the body but he that committed fornication sinneth against his own body." (1 Corinthians 6:18)

"Flee youthful lusts: but follow righteousness, faith, charity, peace, with them that call on the Lord out of a pure heart." (1 Timothy 2:22)

I can still remember when it began. I had reached puberty with its uncertainty and myriad changes, when I found a Penthouse book left in the house by one of my older brothers. The nude picture and stories inside captivated and aroused me. I wanted to experience the sexual pleasures that the various authors talked about.

For the next several years, I found myself trapped and in bondage. I was driven by an inner urge to gratify sexual urges without regard to morality. Whether by masturbation or elicit sexual relationship, I was in bondage to Delilah. I remember in disgust one day grabbing the many Penthouse books and throwing them in the garbage. But the damage had been done, the images had already been imbedded in my spirit. Women had become sexual objects to be used for pleasure and gratification.

It was only after I became a Christian that my sexual desires began healing. Over the years, the Holy Spirit has disciplined me in this area. But even with the disciplining of the Holy Spirit, there must be a constant watch for Delilah. Very crafty, the spirit of Delilah shows up when you least expect it, and when it does, the promise of ecstasy is always there. Just one night in bed will relieve you of all your worries and fears. But she never tells you that you will be embroiled in a bitter divorce and paying alimony, or suffering from AIDS, alone in a hospital, forsaken by family and friends.

Several years ago, a young man told me how he had been tempted to commit adultery and almost fell. However, his particular case really intrigued me. He had a great marriage and a wonderful homemaker wife. In fact, several weeks earlier, he had told me about his wonderful wife. He explained that being a homemaker, she was not "stressed-out" as other career women are and readily satisfied his sexual appetite. So, I was indeed shocked when he told me about his temptation. I encouraged him not to allow the devil to trick him to have an affair, and to remain faithful to his wife. Little did I know that the encouragement was inadequate, until I experienced my own temptation.

A week later, at work, a lady came into my office seeking financial advice. She was attractive and had a very innocent feminine demeanor. Our personalities seemed to "jell," and before I knew it, I felt an attraction. I was a bit baffled at what I was experiencing because I considered myself well-disciplined in this area. After talking some more, we shook hands and she departed. It felt like someone had shocked me with electricity and I went away to the lunchroom and prayed.

That afternoon, I told my wife about the experience. Instead of being upset, she had a good laugh about it. She had always called me a person who seemed to be impervious to temptation and was not like the "ordinary" Christian who may daily struggle with these temptations. So, when I confessed, she laughed and said that I had finally come down to earth.

But my confession and our subsequent conversation after her "good laugh," were like a healing balm. The attraction disappeared, and I learned the secret to defeating Satan in these areas. *"He that covereth his sins shall not prosper: but whoso confesseth and forsaketh them shall have mercy." (Proverbs 28:13) "Confess your faults one to another, and pray one for another, that ye may be help. The effectual fervent prayer of a righteous man availeth much." (James 5:16)*

You see, Satan can't dwell in light. He needs us to hide our mistakes and sins so that the lust becomes stronger and entrenched. The sin seems sweeter and the truth of punishment and consequences for bad behavior are left behind in the distant past. So, when I confessed and opened up about the incident, the psychological attraction and hold was broken. It was just an illusion created in my mind.

As men, we often walk around with our problems masked behind a curtain of self-composure and control. The pride in our lives prevents us from receiving the help and healing that we so desperately need. Help is there for you, but you are too afraid to ask. Let God know what you are feeling. Confess and renounce this impure desire. Be frank and honest. If your wife is a serious and committed Christian, she is the best person to help you. If this avenue will prove detrimental to your marriage, find a Christian counselor who is operating in the Spirit; someone who can discern whether this is just an attraction or a demonic spirit that may need dislodging.

Talking to most men, few understand their sexual power, and still few again understand how to protect their sexuality. God has gifted the male with a strong sexual desire to meet the needs of his helpmeet and for procreation. This wonderful gift from God has been given to him for pleasure and fulfillment. But for most men, their sexual drive has become their Achilles heel because of their inability to properly govern it. Perverse sexual desire is like a floodgate; once it's open, only a miracle can close it back again.

The Bible character Joseph offers an excellent example about handling sexual desire. Almost daily, he was pursued by his employer's wife. But instead of buckling under pressure, he resisted her advances. One day when he was at the office, she tried to rape him. Joseph did what real men do. He rebuked her! Then he ran away, leaving his garment in her hand to ensure that she did not arouse his sexual desires.

Protect your strong God-given sexual drive like gold. Get rid of the pornography in your home: all magazines, videos, statues, all sexual paraphernalia. All! If it's on your Internet, filter it out. Do not give Satan room in your life to use your sexual desire against you. If your sex life in your marriage is dead, let God restore it. There is nothing too hard for Him to do. If He can raise Lazarus from the dead, he can surely restore sexual pleasure to your marriage.

Finally, don't let your eyes constantly wander, checking out the feminine anatomy of other women. There is a natural attraction between women and men, this we cannot run away from. However, we can discipline roving eyes that stop on flesh and park there. Keep moving; if you are parked there for long, you are bound to get a flat tire. A good example of this is when King David saw Bathsheba bathing on her rooftop from the casement of his window. Instead of immediately backing away and doing something else, he decided to keep looking and you know what happened. He got aroused, then enflamed. Eventually, he killed the woman's husband to cover-up his adultery. One time is never enough. Infidelity is alluring and deceptive. You will keep going back for more, eventually destroying yourself. Proverbs describes the scenario like this, *"Hear me now therefore, O ye children, and depart not from the words of my mouth. Remove thy way far from her, and come not nigh the door of her house: Lest thou give thine honor unto others, and thy years unto the cruel: Lest strangers be filled with thy wealth; and thy labors be in the house of a stranger; And thou mourn at the last, when thy flesh and thy body are consumed. And say, How have I hated instruction, and my heart despised reproof..." (Proverbs 5:7-12)*

Remember, you must keep the door to your sexuality shut until your wife knocks. God will honor your discipline and temperance like Joseph. If a man controls his sexuality, it shows maturity and his capacity for responsibility and leadership. Not that this is the only thing that is required for leadership, however, self-control is a level of maturity that every man must achieve if he wants to be a good leader. Many charismatic leaders including King David have caused must reproach on the name of the Lord because they did not tame their sexual desires. However, conquering Delilah is not difficult if we listen to the Holy Spirit and obey Him when He tells us to run.

CHAPTER 6

MAD MAN

The Boeing 737 had hardly touched down on the small remote airstrip when the packed aircraft's boisterous passengers bellowed out their feelings of gratitude to the Bahamasair Pilot. The stormy weather out of Nassau had made the flight turbulent with sharp falls and steep climbs. But the superb skills of the pilot seemed to transcend the angry heavens and brought peace amidst the storm. For most of the passengers, it was their first time in the Bahamas.

Disembarking from the colorful gold and aqua marine airplane, the island visitors slowly made their way to the baggage claim terminal. The sight of the tall coconut trees, endless rows of colorful Poinciana trees, coupled with soft trade winds blowing against their faces enchanted and intoxicated them with feelings of pleasure and euphoria. The exotic island atmosphere had beckoned, and the invitation was accepted. They had come to partake in the wedding ceremony of their friends, Samantha O'Hara and Kevin Lucian.

Both Samantha and Kevin had graduated from Harvard University with honors and were now successfully pursuing careers in pharmaceuticals and business. Kevin secured a middle management post at Meridian Bank, the largest and fastest growing bank in North America. Samantha was hired in a senior supervisory capacity by Global Pharmaceuticals, an international distributor of new innovative drugs that fight cancer. Both made megabucks salaries and with little debt expenditure, they were well on their way to financial prosperity.

Samantha had grown up in the slow and rural outskirts of the South Georgia countryside. Kevin's early life was spent in the busy suburbs of one of New York's urban communities. Despite their different upbringings, they seemed to be the perfect match. Kevin's masculine Italian features complimented Samantha's soft Georgian demeanor. He was ruggedly handsome. She was petite and innocently beautiful. Two days later, they fulfilled their fantasy wedding and were married on the coral pink sands of Harbor Island, Eleuthera in the Bahamas. Then their hell began!

Kevin always felt that Samantha was a bit shy and withdrawn. During their courtship at Harvard, they had kissed and petted often, but Samantha would always pull away before the action got too hot. He thought that it was because she wanted to avoid engaging in any sexual intercourse before marriage. But marriage changed that thought forever. After sexual intercourse each night, Samantha would cry uncontrollably and push him away when he tried to hold her in his arms. At first, he thought that he was doing something wrong. Then she told him the ugly truth: her father and uncle had molested her. Initially, he felt compassionate but after she continued her episodes of crying, he became intolerant and frustrated.

Two weeks after returning home from their honeymoon, Kevin snapped! Something hideous inside him rose up from the dead. He slapped Samantha across the face when she rejected his sexual advances. Though he hated himself for doing it, and the hurt expression on his wife's face filled him with regret, Kevin found himself night after night, physically abusing the woman he had promised to love.

Slapping, jerking and verbally abusing Samantha became an almost daily occurrence. Kevin was trapped by an invisible force that he felt impossible to break. He was reliving the nightmare that he hated so much; the nightmare of seeing his father batter his mother. But what could he do?

He was held hostage by a past that didn't want to let him go. His perfect marriage was quickly unraveling.

After a year of battling, they decided to go for counseling. One of Kevin's co-workers suggested a Christian counselor who had saved his marriage. The first counseling session was explosive, with both blaming the other for their marital problems. But the elderly counselor was persistent and slowly brought out the information from them. Their issues were not external, they were internal, with each unable to heal the wounds they had experienced. If they did not make some changes fast, their marriage would be history. Kevin and Samantha were desperate, they needed help and they needed it now. They had both tried changing before, but it didn't work. But the answer did come, an answer that would radically change their lives forever.

On their second visit for counseling, the elderly counselor took a different approach. He began by asking Kevin and Samantha to forgive the people that had abused and failed them. They both resented the suggestion and balked at this unusual request. Kevin hated his father and Samantha was full of resentment toward her father also. But the earnest persuasive plea of the counselor touched their hearts, and they decided to at least try it. The counseling session ended with prayer and Kevin and Samantha made a commitment and decision to make Jesus the Lord of their lives.

The results were explosive that weekend. They called their parents and explained that they had become Christians and wanted to discuss some things that had happened in the past. The conversations started slowly and cautiously. There were denials and objections, but the truth prevailed. Then, the tears of forgiveness and repentance flowed from parents and children. The wounds that had been opened for so long were now healing. For Kevin and Samantha their marriage seemed to change overnight. The abuse stopped, and their sexual life became normal. Like the day they traveled to the Bahamas, their marriage mounted the sky again and soared to a new height of bliss and fulfillment.

* * *

Statistics indicate that almost sixty percent of married women suffer from some form of abuse in their marriage. I also believe that many men are also suffering from abuse. The harsh reality of these numbers is among those who eventually seek divorce and separation. I believe that most men who commit these abusive acts are confused and ashamed of their behavior. Shackled by a spirit of rage, they vent out destruction in their homes. But they could change and find relief if they are willing to allow the Holy Spirit to intervene in their lives and bring peace like only He can. *"Peace I leave with you, my peace I give unto you: not as the world giveth, give I unto you, Let not your heart be troubled, neither let it be afraid."* (John 15:27)

IS ANGER BAD?

When God placed the emotion of anger in man's biological and psychological make-up, it was a good thing. **God designed anger as a very strong emotion to confront, prevent and vanquish evil.** This emotion is a demonstration of God's mind toward evil: He hates it! In fact, scripture describes God as a man of war. *"The Lord is a man of war the Lord is his name." Exodus 15:3.* Anger is the propelling agent for us to fight evil. Properly regulated in the male psyche, anger is meant to protect and defend his wife and family from danger both physical and spiritual. Excellent examples of this can be found in the Bible's narrative of the lives of King Saul and our Lord Jesus Christ.

"AND, BEHOLD, SAUL CAME AFTER THE HERD OUT OF THE FIELD; AND SAUL SAID, WHAT AILETH THE PEOPLE THAT THEY WEEP? AND THEY TOLD HIM THE TIDINGS OF THE MEN OF JABESH, *AND THE SPIRIT OF GOD CAME UPON SAUL WHEN HE HEARD THOSE TIDINGS, AND HIS ANGER WAS KINDLED GREATLY.* AND HE TOOK A YOKE OF OXEN, AND HEWED THEM IN PIECES, AND SENT THEM THROUGHOUT ALL THE COASTS OF ISRAEL BY THE HANDS OF MESSENGERS, SAYING, WHOSOEVER COMETH NOT FORTH AFTER SAUL AND AFTER SAMUEL SO SHALL IT BE DONE UNTO HIS OXEN, AND THE FEAR OF THE LORD FELL ON

THE PEOPLE, AND THEY CAME OUT WITH ONE CONSENT." (1 SAMUEL 11:5-7)

"AND THE JEWS' PASSOVER WAS AT HAND, AND JESUS WENT UP TO JERUSALEM, AND FOUND IN THE TEMPLE THOSE THAT SOLD OXEN AND SHEEP AND DOVES, AND THE CHANGERS OF MONEY SITTING: AND WHEN HE HAD MADE A SCOURGE OF SMALL CORDS; HE DROVE THEM ALL OUT OF THE TEMPLE, AND THE SHEEP, AND THE OXEN; AND POURED OUT THE CHANGERS' MONEY, AND OVERTHREW THE TABLES; AND SAID UNTO THEM THAT SOLD DOVES, "TAKE THESE THINGS HENCE; MAKE NOT MY FATHER'S HOUSE AN HOUSE OF MERCHANDISE." AND HIS DISCIPLES REMEMBERED THAT IT WAS WRITTEN, "THE ZEAL OF THINE HOUSE HATH EATEN ME UP." (JOHN 2:13-17)

In each case, we can see that anger was a demonstration of God's will. God wanted Saul to conquer Israel's enemies. Jesus' anger supported God's purity and obedience when it comes to use of His house. In neither case was there uncontrollable venting of personal animosity and ill feelings. This is the big difference between good anger and bad anger. One is vented because of flesh, pride and desire for control, while the other is displayed under the guidance of the Holy Spirit and a desire for righteousness.

When a person is displaying his anger under the guidance of the Holy Spirit, he can indeed *"be angry and sin not." (Ephesians 4:26)* His flesh is not active and influencing his actions. On the other hand, if a person's anger is controlled by his flesh and a need to dominate others, abuse, whether verbal or physical can take place. Anger is a very strong passion and the Bible strictly admonishes that one should not be hasty to be angry. *"Be not hasty in thy spirit to be angry: for anger resteth in the bosom of fools." Ecclesiastes 7:9 "Cease from anger, and forsake wrath: fret not thyself in any wise to do evil." Psalm 37:8 "He that is slow to anger is better than the mighty; and he that ruleth his spirit than the that taketh a city." Proverbs 16:32*

There are times in all our lives when the need to display anger is necessary. There are times when I have seen the poor overlooked and disregarded by the community and churches and it makes me angry. When the word of God is misinterpreted and used to bring God's people into bondage instead of liberty, a fire of anger ignites in my spirit. There are times when my wife has done things contrary to sound judgment or set down rules that have made me angry.

I believe that this is the type of anger that we should have. In fact, I wish the whole church would get angry with the devil and pray until the demons of cancer, oppression in every form, and poverty are totally vanquished from the earth. We need anger that motivates us for justice and righteousness. All the great men in history who fought for justice and righteousness were motivated by this *good* anger.

When our children are disobedient and have disobeyed family or public rules and ethics, depending on the infraction displaying anger is in order and quite natural. I am not talking about uncontrollable anger where we just want to lash out without regard for safety of the child or the emotional damage that we will do to them. In these circumstances, we must determine our response based on the infraction and its severity. In these cases, whether it's a simple verbal reprimand or paddling, the response is predetermined and totally under our control. In fact, this response will build confidence in our children as they behold our composed behavior in discipline.

PAST ABUSE

"MAKE NO FRIENDSHIP WITH AN ANGRY MAN; AND WITH A FURIOUS MAN THOU SHALT NOT GO; LEST THOU LEARN HIS WAYS, AND GET A SNARE TO THY SOUL." (PROVERBS 22:24-25)

It is a known fact that persons who come from abusive homes, usually become abusers themselves. Why? Shouldn't they after having seen the devastation that abuse can cause, avoid it at all costs? I believe in rare cases those people who have seen and experienced abuse learn to avoid it, however, statistics indicate that in most cases people who have experienced abuse perpetuate it in their own families. Why? The root of abuse is usually passed on from one generation to another. There are several root components that cause men to resort to abuse: pride, unforgiveness, demonic spirits and impatience. If these components are not removed from an individual's life, abuse in some form will flourish.

For most people as aforesaid, their abuse is usually bequeathed to them as a result of being born into an abusive environment. The damage is done in two ways. First, by viewing the abuse, their spirits become infected by the images that they see. Then, by holding unforgiveness against the person who perpetrated the abuse, they open the door for bitterness to ferment and demonic spirits to inhabit their hearts.

To avoid this horrific dilemma from happening or to prevent its continuation in your life, you must repent, renounce and forgive. First confess your abusive ways and ask God to forgive you. This must not be done in a half-hearted way. There must be genuine contrition and a deliberate effort to turn away from the abusive behavior. Renounce and recognize it for what it is: unhealthy and ungodly. Lastly, you must forgive the person who perpetrated the abuse against you. You must let it go! If you don't, it will continue to live within you, and remain an open door for demons to control and manipulate your emotions and behavior.

When people grow up in families where abuse is a constant part of their lives there is always the possibility that demonic spirits are present in that environment. And in a lot of cases, the demonic spirits are transferred to the children of the abusers. Unaware of the spirits' intrusion in their lives, when the children become parents themselves, they become abusers influenced by these demonic spirits. In this case, the demon spirit must be dislodged by the power of the Holy Spirit. This needs done through fasting and prayer by a Holy Spirit filled individual.

WILLFUL PRIDE

"Only by pride cometh contention: but with the well advised is wisdom." (Proverbs 13:10)

"Proud and haughty scorner is his name, who dealeth
in proud wrath." (Proverbs 21:24)

"In the mouth of the foolish is a rod of pride: but the
lips of the wise shall preserve them." (Proverbs 14:3)

Uncontrollable anger is the rod of willful pride, and a major reason why anger lingers in the lives of Christians. But this is not the type of pride that is easily detected or cured because of its deceptive nature. Most people believe pride and arrogance is thinking that you are better than other people. However, pride goes much deeper that this. Pride also means independence and self-centeredness. Instead of submitting to God in true humility, you have become a law unto yourself. Thus, you are a very willful individual who is easily agitated when things don't go your way. You are argumentative and impatient with people because you believe that you are cleverer, more intelligent, better informed and superior to them.

This type of anger dominated King Saul. Saul's pride eventually caused his rejection by God which opened the door for him to be possessed by a demonic spirit of violence.

"For rebellion is as the sin of witchcraft, and
stubbornness is as iniquity and idolatry. Because
thou has rejected the word of the Lord, he hath also
rejected thee from being king." (1 Samuel 15:23)

"But the Spirit of the Lord departed from Saul, and
an evil spirit from the Lord troubled him." (1 Samuel
16:8)

"And it came to pass on the morrow, that the evil
spirit from God came upon Saul, and be prophesied
in the midst of the house: and David played with his
hand, as at other times: and there was a javelin in
Saul's hand. And Saul cast the javelin; for he said, I
will smite David even to the wall with it. And David
avoided out of his presence twice." (1 Samuel 18:10-11)

King Saul was a very willful individual who always found a reason for not obeying God. God was late. God's way was not the best way. Praise from people was better than obeying God and so on. Saul's willfulness eventually caused him to lose the anointing and brought judgment on his whole family. Willful pride is extremely subtle and usually lives on in people until they give themselves without reservation to God. This is the secret sin that David spoke about in the Psalms, "Who can understand his errors? Cleanse thou me from secret faults. Keep back thy servant also from presumptuous sins; let them not have dominion over me: then shall I be upright, and I shall be innocent from the great transgression." Psalm 19:12-13

You must allow the Holy Spirit to wash you from this secret sin. He has promised to perfect that which concerns you. This means that he is responsible for restoring and refurbishing your soul. This may take some time. However, God is faithful and will not disappoint you. But let me encourage you: pride must be broken. God will put you through circumstances to break the pride from your life. And when He puts you in the washing machine no matter how painful, don't try to come out. Stay in the machine until all the cycles are finished.

I believe this is the type of pride that plagues most men, including me. Even after becoming a Christian, I found myself being subjected to loud outbursts and arguments with my wife and others. Although I never allowed arguments to be reduced to physical abuse, the strife and need for control were there. Even after confession and prayer, the uncontrollable anger continued. It would go away for a time then return with a vengeance.

It wasn't until God finally delivered me from male pride that the anger finally dissipated. Wow! What relief! The reason I didn't get relief right away was because I was treating the symptom instead of the actual disease. Now, I find my anger being properly calibrated by the Holy Spirit; anger to withstand the Hordes of Hell; anger to walk out in faith when the Devil says it won't work. I'm not perfect, no, but with God's grace, I am heading in the right direction.

THE ROAD TO MATURITY

INTRODUCTION

For most men, the image of a mature man has been severely distorted and skewed by our favorite hero on TV or in the movies. Coupled with that, most fathers especially in the Western world have absolutely no clue about patriarchy and the powerful truth of leaving a spiritual legacy.

In these last days of much evil, deceit, and selfishness, our psyche has been inundated with either charismatic men who through their clever words and thinking get the job done; or men who have given in to so-called "strong" female leadership out of false equality and what is best.

These lies perpetuated by the prince of darkness, are designed to keep men from reaching their goals of maturity. When a man knows who he is and can mentor others, he can change his household, his community and his nation. Abraham did that. He left a legacy that our Lord Jesus Christ was born into. Abraham was a man of faith, obedience and *patience; the mark of true maturity.*

His maturity led him to leave family and friends to seek God in a far land. His unselfishness, care and sensitivity saved the life of his nephew and moved him to be tender to his wife. Finally, his patience released the ultimate miracle of a son born in very old age. Abraham was indeed a mature man who was called the friend of God.

CHAPTER 7

IT'S OKAY TO BE SENSITIVE

Scripture says, *"Let nothing be done through strife or vainglory; but in lowliness of mind let each esteem other better than themselves." (Philippians 2:3)* Here lies the basis and foundation of sensitivity: stop thinking only about you. Give self a rest. We are all in this together, whether we like it or not, and we need one another. We need people. Like the old adage says, "no man is an island" and the sooner we can understand and embrace that concept, the sooner we can reach a lot of our goals.

One of the best basketball players of all times, Michael Jordan, found himself playing for many years and still had not attained his ultimate goal of an NBA championship. He had to re-valuate his strategy. Yes, he was the best player in the league with exceptional basketball skills, but without the proper supporting cast, he was unable to succeed.

He needed that right supporting teammates to make a title run. The Bulls management embraced this concept and traded for a few talented players that included Scottie Pippen and Dennis Rodman. Scottie Pippen was a player with basketball skills much like Jordan. They also traded for Dennis Rodman who was the best rebounder in the league.

Jordan would not be able to have the forty-point games that he was used to. He had to share the point totals with Pippen, but the team began to win at an unprecedented rate and eventually had the best winning season up to that time. They not only won one championship, they won several in succession.

Without a proper understanding of teamwork and team principles, we may have some success, but the more prestigious goals become elusive. We must remember that there is no "I" in team and Together, Everyone, Achieves, More (TEAM). A man who refuses to acknowledge the gifts and talents of others and especially his wife will fail to achieve those coveted goals of a richer and better family life. Being sensitive doesn't mean we become homosexual or feminine, it means we honor, respect and embrace the gifts of others.

This team first attitude fosters trust and growth in others. It lets them know that they are important and their contributions matter. We do this by listening and valuing their opinion. We may not see or understand at the time what they may be saying, however, listening with an undivided attention validates them as an equal, and as an important contributor.

TRUST, TRANSPARENCY AND COMMUNICATION - KEYS TO UNITY

Nothing can ever take the place of trust as the foundation to unity and friendship. Without trust, we are simply having a symbiotic relationship without any real and genuine cohesiveness. Symbiotic means we have a symbol, an illusion of something real. When a husband and wife have a symbiotic relationship, he may be supplying money and she supplies sexual pleasure. Or, he gives her status and she plays the role of a beautiful and clever wife.

However, without trust, the relationship is not genuine because the two people's hearts are not one. Trust puts everything on the line. Trust says, "Whether I get the money or not I will still love you. Whether we live in a palace or a tiny cottage, I will still love you. When you get old and your beauty is diminished, I will love you even more." The relationship is not based on feelings or physical attributes of money and looks. It's based on genuine trust that grows into a deep love.

It's only after we have learned to trust that true intimacy can begin. We can now reveal our hearts. Scripture says that Adam and Eve were naked and unashamed. This spoke not only about their physical nakedness but also of their spiritual nakedness. They were transparent. There were no lies. No one was trying to manipulate or dominate the other person. They existed to love and serve each other. **This was the original plan of relationship between a man and woman.**

When sin entered the world, then came the notion that I need to hide my true motives. I need to hide my mistakes and shortcomings. I must hide my need to have dominion over people. So, we are afraid of transparency because we will be outed and seen for who we are. Wow! This is the reason the world lives in darkness and people fear being truthful and real; their evil plans and bad hearts will come to light!

For man to truly communicate and truly be an effective leader and responsible, he must come to the light. He must repent! He must acknowledge that he is a sinner. He must bring his will to God for readjustment and training. Transparency is admission that we are nothing and need the Lord for everything. We need His grace to wash our hearts from sin. We need Him to guide and direct us. We need Him to open our minds and hearts to His wisdom.

You see, without transparency we cower and our fears and insecurities forbid us from admitting our faults and shortcomings. Thus, we become incapable of true and genuine communication. Our communication is based on a need to get something and not to give our hearts and lives to another. We want others to see us in a good light, so we can trick, connive and have dominion over others. It's all about us. So true!

The purpose of true communication is unity and oneness. We want people to know us and we them. It is one of the most important building blocks to a successful relationship. However, most people don't communicate; they really don't interact at all. To truly interact, there must be a level of sensitivity and desire to give. We talk or gesture to express ourselves and to understand others. It's a two-way street. However, genuine communication doesn't start with our words. It starts with observation and listening. We must listen, observe and evaluate before we open our mouths to commune with others. And, of course, that requires a whole lot of care and sensitivity.

Many times in my marriage, I was advised and confronted by my wife with regard to issues that we were facing or situations that were going on in our home. Most of the time, I became irritable because I thought she was trying to control me or my male pride didn't want to admit that her ideas were better. So, my responses were at best insensitive and disjointed.

Just before Kim and I got married, she bought several books for both of us to learn about lovemaking. She was a virgin, but I'd had several sexual experiences before we got married, so I thought I really didn't need any help. I was glad she did. The books helped both of us to enjoy our honeymoon and lovemaking throughout our marriage.

In another incident, Kim was almost teary when she warned me not to trust a certain individual. This particular person had done some work for us, however, the work was not complete and they were demanding a part of the money. Flowing in my ultra-male pride, I downplayed my wife's advice, and gave into their demands. I would live to regret it.

The next week, I was out of money and betrayed by the person. I was ashamed. I didn't know how to tell her that I couldn't get the money back. How could I have been so blind! My lack of communication and sensitivity led to bad judgement. I didn't listen and couldn't benefit from the timely advice given to me. Something rooted deep inside me was shutting off my divine supply of wisdom and understanding.

To truly be an effective communicator starts with understanding and listening and not with scornful words that say, "I am the smarter one." We understand who we are talking to and we respect and value their opinions. As a result, our response is flavored with care and humility. However, this is very difficult if the pride and arrogance has not been broken in our lives. When we think that we are better and smarter; when we think that our gender makes us superior; true communication is almost impossible.

Lurking deep within every male is a spiritual octopus that prevents communication and unity with others. And, just like an octopus, the tentacles spread to all facets of a man's life choking and preventing him from being sensitive to others, clouding his judgement and making him obstinate to the Holy Spirit. Here is a list of these spiritual tentacles:

Pride – arrogant, independent, self-worship and willfulness that refuses to listen or take advice from others

Insensitive/Callous – having an attitude devoid of compassion and feelings for one's wife and others

Domination – oppressive and wanting to have one's way in every situation

Control – never giving others the freedom to choose/must have mastery of others/manipulative

Dishonor/Condescending – a judgmental attitude that grades others as less than oneself/unable to see the equality of mankind or to esteem others as better than oneself

Superiority – akin to dishonor and condescending, believing one is better because of education, status, race or gender

Analytical – Having a regimental approach to life devoid of faith and good judgement or belief that there is a God and some things are beyond our understanding. Withstands the true move of the Holy Spirit

Slothfulness – Doing things at one's own pace, indifference to the needs of others, also fearful and afraid of tackling and confronting challenges

These tentacles are aggressive, deadly, and constantly preventing a man from being effective and sensitive to others. When he gets one off another one comes to replace it. The biggest problem with these tentacles and the reason men struggle with this octopus that dwells in the deep recesses of his spirit is because it feels so so (purposely repeated) good. The feeling of superiority and being the best is the fuel and food that drives and keeps men in bondage to this creature called male pride.

It's the reason we love our sports where winning is everything. It's the reason we struggle with racism and gender disrespect. We must be the best! Nothing wrong with striving for excellence, however, when it's at the expense of morality, abuse and subjugation of others driven by pride, it's a cancer that eventually destroys our relationship with God and others.

These tentacles are the reason for the wars in the world; wars between husbands and wives, siblings, political parties, ethnicities and countries. The driving force is always pride; the spirit of Satan and his avenue to keep men walking in delusion believing absolute nonsense and bringing death and destruction to themselves and those with whom they come into contact.

Without grace and humility, a man becomes isolated and insulated against change, growth and meeting the needs of others; especially his wife. Because he sees himself as being better and superior, he magnifies her mistakes; he belittles her emotional disposition; he procrastinates with her requests. His logic is king and his regimental and analytical approach makes conversation, teamwork and unity impossible.

The second greatest commandment is to love thy neighbor as oneself. And, the parable of the Good Samaritan is the epitome of how we should treat others: with an attitude of care and sensitivity. Like a popular adage that says, "We should never look down at another man unless we are lifting him up." This would motivate a man to look for opportunities to spend time with his wife; buy her gifts; take her on vacation; meet her sexual needs by being sensitive in the bedroom. Life no longer revolves around "me." Scripture says, *"But I would have you without carefulness.*

He that is unmarried careth for the things that belong to the Lord, how he may please the Lord: But he that is married careth for the things that are of the world, how he may please his wife." (1 Corinthian 7:32-33)

Loving people is the antidote for insensitivity and callousness. It's not always bad choices that have people financially bankrupt or suffering in a bad relationship. Life throws punches at all of us in different ways. Some people are born into poverty. Others have sickness and diseases come their way. And, like the insensitive friends of Job, who mercilessly told him that his dilemma was a result of his hidden sins, many people fail to extend mercy or a helping hand to those experiencing the worst of life.

However, if we have a sensitive and caring heart, we feel, we sympathize, we understand and most of all, it propels us to action. After seeing the man on the side of the road bruised and beaten, the Good Samaritan carried him to a place for shelter and healing. The Priest and Levite, who should have been sensitive, walked by on the other side. They were immune to the need of another because their religious and self-righteous spirit told them that the man deserved his misfortune because of some bad thing that he had done.

MEETING HER NEEDS

"Likewise, ye husbands, dwell with them according to knowledge giving honour unto the wife, as unto the weaker vessel, and as being heirs together of the grace of life, that your prayers be not hindered." (1 Peter 3:7)

"But he that is married careth for the things that are of the world, how he may please his wife." (1 Corinthians 7:32)

"Husbands, love your wives, even as Christ also loved the church, and gave himself for it." (Ephesians 5:25)

"So ought men to love their wives as their own bodies. He that loveth his wife loveth himself." (Ephesians 5:28)

"Nevertheless let every one of you in particular so love his wife even as himself; and the wife see that she reverence her husband." (Ephesians 5:33)

We must always resist this callous attitude that looks for reasons not to help. In fact, scripture tells us to bear each other's burdens and not be selfish. *"Bear ye one another's burdens, and so fulfil the law of Christ."* *(Galatians 6:2)* *"Look not every man on his own things, but every man also on the things of others."* *(Philippians 2:4)* A man who has reached this level of maturity will find it very easy to connect with people. They know he truly cares about them.

When a husband demonstrates to his wife this level of sensitivity, as some psychologists would say that, he is in touch with his feminine side. Her emotions and disposition are no longer foolish. He is patient and understanding. He is gentle and tender toward her, acknowledging the difference between the sexes. He doesn't become feminine; he becomes tender, patient and understanding. He humbles himself to touch her spirit and see things through her eyes.

The female spirit is nurtured and refreshed by his tender and unselfish approach. A woman is free to be herself and not feel forced into being another male. This tender disposition silences her fears and breaks down the doors of insecurities that separate the genders. This man of tenderness and feelings creates an insatiable desire for his presence and closeness. He becomes the sweet flavor that her heart constantly longs for.

The gentle and tender approach is the sweetness that the Shulamite woman found in Solomon. She was in love with the sweetness of his character which naturally resulted in passionate lovemaking. *"Let him kiss me with the kisses of his mouth: for thy love is better than wine."* *(Songs of Solomon 1:2)* *"By night on my bed I sought him whom my soul loveth: I sought him, but I found him not. I will rise now, and go about the city in the streets, and in the broad ways I will seek him whom my soul loveth: I sought him, but I found him not. The watchmen that go about the city found me: to whom I said, Saw ye him whom my soul loveth? It was but a little that I passed from them, but I found him whom my soul loveth: I held him, and would not let him go, until I had brought him into my mother's house, and into the chamber of her that conceived me. I charge you, O ye daughters of Jerusalem, by the roes, and by the hinds of the field, that ye stir not up, nor awake my love, till he please." (Songs of Solomon 3:1-5)*

For a man to tap into this dimension, he must be willing to sacrifice time and his own personal ambitions. I have heard many men proclaim, "I paid the bills…what more does she want." Whereas paying the bills does alleviate some stress, it can't substitute for unselfish love. I know at times we need our space to enjoy our hobbies, friends and our own time with the Lord. But let us remember why we are in a relationship: to serve.

Some of the most enjoyable times of my life have been just spending time talking and getting to know each other. Some nights, Kim and I would talk until the wee morning hours. We talked about current events, our children, church, and revelations from the Lord and so on. Our conversations relieved tensions and cultivated intimacy. And, after each conversation, we felt the walls between us had broken down and we experienced the closeness of true friendship. Then, we could fall asleep wrapped in each other's arms…after, of course, some heated passion!

CHAPTER 8

THE HEART OF A FATHER

Amos walked slowly into the huge dome-shaped tabernacle. It was magnificent! Although it was made with modern twenty-first century material, the structural style was vintage Roman architecture. The arches, the classic Michelangelo sculptures of Mary, Jesus and other Bible figures made the New Northern Church of the Living God, simply breathtaking! But today, Reverend Doctor Amos Cathison's mind was far from church or any ecclesiastical reflections. He was disturbed and perplexed by the tumultuous events that were happening at home. His marriage of twenty-seven years was falling apart.

Amos had graduated Valedictorian from one of America's most exclusive religious universities. He was the President of both the college newspaper and the student counsel committee. He was also voted most likely to succeed by his fellow graduates and several times during his time at the university, he was featured in the "Who's Who in American Colleges and Universities" magazine. Upon graduation, success seemed to overwhelm him. He was immediately invited to become an associate Pastor at a large prestigious church where he quickly excelled.

Through his expertise, the Church grew rapidly and shortly afterward, Amos decided to start his own congregation. His great oratory skills and witty humor soon garnered a large following at the New Northern church of the Living God. Church membership mushroomed, and a site was selected for the new domed church. Wealth, fame and prosperity became his almost overnight. But beneath the veneer of success and self-confidence, a spiritual cancer had developed which rapidly spread to all areas of his life.

Family life at the Cathison home resembled a miniature Auschwitz where Amos the Terrible ruled with an iron fist. He was dreaded by everyone in the house. He treated the children like boot camp recruits, constantly pushing them to succeed but rarely giving them encouragement or showing compassion. His children resented him and rarely approached him for advice or direction in their lives. Their only wish was a quick exit from the Cathison concentration camp. Managing the church's office was more important to Amos than spending quality time with his wife or family.

The one who suffered the most was Gail. Quiet and faithful, she felt the door of claustrophobia slam shut the day she married the illustrious Reverend. She was the one who bore the brunt of his insensitivity, especially after he had delivered his most stirring sermons. This was when he was most intolerable. He would magnify her mistakes and make a mockery of her intelligence and suggestions. The good "Rev" was a modern-day Pharisee, appearing good on the outside but inwardly corrupt. The ugly demon of religiosity had taken possession of his life.

But Amos's wakeup call came the night before when he humiliated Gail for preparing dinner later than his 5 p.m. mealtime. It was the straw that broke the camel's back. Gail exploded! Yelling at the top of her lungs, "I'm tired of this make-believe life! It's all a lie! I can't do this anymore! I hate you! I want a divorce!" She had finally had enough. She was tired of being put on the back burner; tired of being treated like a piece of furniture. She was tired too of being a doormat and being short-changed in the name of religion. She felt used and betrayed.

Amos was devastated. What would he do? His reputation was at stake. Shame and disgrace were imminent. And today, as he prepared to enter the sanctuary to begin preaching his six-part series sermon on "The Keys to Success in Christianity;" now he felt so empty and inadequate. But even then, the truth still eluded the illustrious Reverend. His main interest was saving face and not saving his marriage. His main interest was keeping the fame, fortune and prestige. Silly "Rev," the deadly cancer of religiosity had deceived him and caused him to miss the pure sweetness of marriage, family life and possibly heaven.

* * *

"KEEPING MERCY FOR THOUSANDS, FORGIVING INIQUITY AND TRANSGRESSION AND SIN, AND THAT WILL BY NO MEANS CLEAR *THE GUILTY;* VISITING THE INIQUITY OF THE FATHERS UPON THE CHILDREN, AND UPON THE CHILDREN'S CHILDREN, UNTO THE THIRD AND TO THE FOURTH *GENERATION.*" (EXODUS 34:7)

"KNOW THEREFORE THAT THE LORD THY GOD, HE IS GOD, THE FAITHFUL GOD, WHICH KEEPETH COVENANT AND MERCY WITH THEM THAT LOVE HIM AND KEEP HIS COMMANDMENTS TO A THOUSAND GENERATIONS;" (DEUTERONOMY 7:9)

"THOU SHALT NOT BOW DOWN THYSELF UNTO THEM, NOR SERVE THEM: FOR I THE LORD THY GOD AM A JEALOUS GOD, VISITING THE INIQUITY OF THE FATHERS UPON THE CHILDREN UNTO THE THIRD AND FOURTH GENERATION OF THEM THAT HATE ME," (DEUTERONOMY 5:9)

What an awful legacy for a man to leave his family. He allowed popularity, fame and greed to deceive him from fulfilling his true purpose of father and husband. The very essence of authority and patriarchy demands that a man invest in his family. What he leaves behind reveals his true character and person. In fact, a lot of who we are or what we will become comes from our ancestors both genetically and spiritually.

Both our mistakes and our successes impact our families for generations. A simple example could be a man who incurred large debts and dies without life insurance. If he has a wife and family, the debts fall to his estate. The creditors look for ways to collect by imposing liens on properties and bank accounts. The family in turn must wait until these liabilities are settled before collecting their depleted inheritance.

The same is true of the man who was an adulterer and has children outside his marriage. These illegitimate children are often treated with contempt even though they are not at fault. His sin of adultery is bequeathed to the "outside" children. Contra wise, a man of good character bequeaths his good name to his children who gain favor and goodwill from people who they don't even know just because the father handled his business interests and people with honesty and integrity.

Of course, the best and greatest way to impact our future generations is by our faith and obedience to God. The Jewish nation to this day still benefits from the life of a man called Abraham. His faith and obedience to God gained blessings from God for all their generations. "*As concerning the gospel, they are enemies for your sakes: but as touching the election, **they are beloved for the fathers' sakes.**" (Roman 11:28)* "*I have been young, and now am old; yet have I not seen the righteous forsaken, nor his seed begging bread.*" (Psalm 37:25)

That is why the devil continues to confuse patriarchal authority. When men and fathers don't understand that they represent a gate and doorway to their families because of their God-given authority, they do their families and generations a great spiritual injury. By disobeying God's word, they, like Adam, give the devil legitimate right and leverage to oppress and dominate their families.

Many children operate under a curse without even realizing it. They are not aware that the money, family, divorce and other problems they have, were passed on to them before they were even born. They were passed on by a father who rejected and disobeyed God's laws and spiritual instructions. Sad, but true. If you understand this profound truth, then you should endeavor to impact your generations by living a Godly life of faith and obedience to God's word.

THE FIRST PRINCIPLE OF FATHERHOOD - COMPASSION

"AND HE AROSE, AND CAME TO HIS FATHER. BUT WHEN HE
WAS YET A GREAT WAY OFF, HIS FATHER SAW HIM, AND HAD
COMPASSION, AND RAN, AND FELL ON HIS NECK, AND KISSED
HIM. AND THE SON SAID UNTO HIM, FATHER, I HAVE SINNED
AGAINST HEAVEN, AND IN THY SIGHT, AND AM NO MORE
WORTHY TO BE CALLED THY SON. BUT THE FATHER SAID TO
HIS SERVANTS, BRING FORTH THE BEST ROBE, AND PUT IT ON
HIM; AND PUT A RING ON HIS HAND, AND SHOES ON HIS FEET:
AND BRING HITHER THE FATTED CALF, AND KILL IT; AND LET
US EAT, AND BE MERRY: FOR THIS MY SON WAS DEAD, AND IS
ALIVE AGAIN; HE WAS LOST, AND IS FOUND. AND THEY BEGAN
TO BE MERRY." (MATTHEW 15:20-24)

"BE YE THEREFORE MERCIFUL, AS YOUR FATHER ALSO IS
MERCIFUL." (LUKE 6:36)

I do not think that there is any single verse or passage of scripture that vividly reveals the heart of God, the Father, as powerfully as the above parable. God is love. Plain and simple, He is love. He desperately wants to be reunited and fellowship with His creation. He wants to bless His creation with the very best. He wants us to rejoice together. The reason, we as Christians, still live in the back alley of poverty, distress and unbelief is because we don't know the heart of the Father. Love that spans the universe yet meticulously looks into every detail of our lives.

Prior to Jesus coming, the people of God had a very limited revelation of God. They knew God as the provider, Jehovah Jerih who provided a ram in the thicket for Abraham. He provided food in the wilderness when the Israelites left Egypt and came into the Promised Land. They knew Him as Jehovah Shamah, the Lord who is always there. They knew Him as Jehovah, the dreadful God of judgment who almost erased Egypt from the face of the earth, but none knew him as the Father longing to have a relationship; a Father that loved His creation so much that He would send His only Son to die for them. *"For God so loved the world that he gave his only begotten son that whosoever believeth in him would not perish but have everlasting life." (John 3:16)*

Most people would agree that this is one of the most profound scriptures in the Bible, yet few have experienced the dynamics of the Father's love in their own heart, a torrential love that is actively pursuing fellowship with the human soul. As a father, we must take our cue from our Heavenly Father's example. We must do everything within our power to connect and bond with our families. We must demonstrate a life of care, compassion, forgiveness and fellowship. We must approach our families with a heart that is willing to go the farthest mile in forgiveness and willing to sacrifice time and energy. We must turn away from the cold callous pride that makes us unforgiving, rigid, and alienates us from our families.

Our families need love more than the harsh words and critical overbearing attitude. They need love more than the condescending and analytical approach. They need someone who looks beyond their faults and sees their needs. God wants to save His people, not condemn and destroy them; this is the Father's heart. A father's words, actions, discipline, must all be done in an effort to heal the wounds of insecurity that they have and those that life constantly inflicts upon them.

For example, my youngest daughter seemed to have a will of her own. As you may know, the disciplinarian in me wanted to tame that little will. I wanted to put her on my discipline farm until I could see some positive growth. But, this is not God's way. Her strong will and forward ways were a result of her insecurities. She thought that I loved my oldest daughter more than her and she needed to protect herself and strive for more attention. God's insight; she needs more love and bonding, not harsh correction. She needed freedom and nurturing. When I obeyed God's voice, the changes were dramatic and swift. She began to bond with me.

Lack of bonding has been the mistake of most fathers including me. We neglect to bond before we teach. We forget to connect before lead. We avoid a relationship before we correct. Bonding and connecting silence the fears and erase the insecurities that keep children from trusting.

Bonding means that forgiveness and love are freely given even when errors and bad judgments are made. People hear better and develop faster when they have learned to trust. A father must gently and gradually connect with his children, building the relationship on a foundation of love. Then, he can lead, teach and correct with authority and confidence. The bond of friendship and love is secure enough to take the chaffing of the learning and development stage of life.

This, of course, is not easy to do. I remember scolding my son for something he had done. I wanted him to understand and implement in his life the advice that I was giving him. But, I could see and sense the resentment and fear in his eyes. My coarse and domineering approach was producing the opposite of what I desired, and instead I was alienating myself from him.

Again, I am grateful for the grace of God tugging at my heart and the inner voice telling me that I must decrease in order for him to increase. God was putting the brakes on my domineering approach to parenthood. In order for me to develop, I would have to daily release him into the hands of the Lord. This is perhaps one of the hardest things for a good father to do, but it is the only way to reap spiritual increase for our children.

In many ways, we try to live our lives through them. However, God's plan is much better. We can plant, we can water, but it's the Lord that gives the increase. A farmer who harvests his crop early and forces it to mature, will have an inferior product. Likewise, a father who is impatient, domineering and controlling will only produce an insecure, people-pleaser who doesn't have the faith and courage to meet life's challenges. We must release our children to the Lord and allow them gradually the freedom of choice. You see, when we love and care, we allow liberty.

"Wait a minute," you may say. "If I give my child too much freedom they will make horrible mistakes." True. In the same vein, their mistakes sometimes are their greatest teachers. The father in the above parable wanted his son to stay at home but his love allowed him the liberty of making his own choice. People who control and oppress their children only heighten insecurities. God doesn't want people to make bad choices and mistakes but neither does He want robots serving Him. If a man chooses to serve God, he inherits the blessing. If he chooses to disobey God, he inherits the curse. He must choose! He should also learn from his mistakes.

Children that grow up in homes with an over-protective parent usually become spiritual and emotional invalids as adults. When or if they move out on their own, their very diminished and inadequate decision-making skills make them very vulnerable and ill-prepared for an incredibly deceptive and harsh world. Some become very wild and loose in their behavior because they were not used to freedom. Others retreat inwardly and become even more emotionally dependent. They simply lack the competence, confidence and maturity to make wise decisions.

God wants us to nurture our children with His insight and wisdom. He knows their hearts and future, and He wants the human father to depend on Him for guidance. We can only do this through prayer and patience. Like different species of plants that require different methods of nurturing, each child is different and requires a different approach and different method of caring. God does not want us to shape them into automatons and religious people that have learned to hide in darkness because of insecurities and fear.

The purpose of fatherhood is to bring about fellowship as our children bask in a secure environment. They are to be nurtured and cared for building their faith and confidence in God. Our joy and peace come when they learn to trust the Lord for themselves and experience His grace and wisdom. A father who demonstrates care and concern for his children ensures the proper development of these precious plants and they reap the rewards.

Some of the most pleasurable times in my family were the times during summer when I would be home on vacation. It was pure joy to prepare food, take them out driving, vacations, or just spend times chatting. Allowing them to voice their opinions and ask questions about God, the Bible and things that interested them gave me the opportunity to connect and provide guidance. I showed them that I cared and valued their friendship. They were important. Over the years, I have watched them grow by leaps and bounds. They have confidence in God and respect for authority. Although they also have made mistakes, the foundation of faith and confidence that comes from a caring father, continues to guide them.

FAITHFULNESS

"GOD IS FAITHFUL, BY WHOM YE WERE CALLED UNTO THE FELLOWSHIP OF HIS SON, JESUS CHRIST OUR LORD." (1 CORINTHIANS 1:9)

"NOW THEREFORE THAT THE LORD THY GOD, HE IS GOD, THE FAITHFUL GOD, WHICH KEEPETH COVENANT AND MERCY WITH THEM THAT LOVE HIM AND KEEP HIS COMMANDMENTS TO A THOUSAND GENERATIONS." (DEUTERONOMY 7:9)

"MOST MEN WILL PROCLAIM EVERYONE HIS OWN GOODNESS: BUT A FAITHFUL MAN WHO CAN." (PROVERBS 20:6)

"AND THE THINGS THAT THOU HAST HEARD OF ME AMONG MANY WITNESSES, THE SAME COMMIT THOU TO FAITHFUL MEN, WHO SHALL BE ABLE TO TEACH OTHERS ALSO." (1 TIMOTHY 2:2)

Nothing I think has devastated the human family more than unfaithfulness. Whether it's adultery, separation, divorce or lack of fulfilling basic promises, fathers breed insecurities into the lives of their children when they break their promises and live selfishly. Father represent head, source, beginning and authority, thus, he is the spiritual conscience of the family. He is the beginning of their image of right, wrong, equity and judgment. By his life living, he ultimately impacts the very mechanism of spiritual and moral awareness of his family including his wife.

When a father is unfaithful, he subconsciously inundates his family with seeds of insecurities that eventually grow into destructive selfish habits. When people are insecure, they find it difficult to form close relationships. They resort to control, manipulation and domination to substitute for genuine trust and transparency. Insecure people live in a world of delusion, where they are only concerned about how they appear to others, rather than the truth about themselves and how they really feel inside. Their lives become a maze of pride and fear struggling to make sense of reality. Insecurity makes us defensive as we view life from a filter of distrust. We perceive advice as accusation and offensive; offered help as demeaning and intrusive. All because, "No one was or is there for me; I don't trust anyone, and I need to take care of myself."

Insecurity started in the Garden of Eden when Adam chose knowledge over a solid relationship with God. He filled us his offspring with insecurity as he broke fellowship. Adam was unfaithful to God, the one who created and loved him. As a result, his off-spring were born into this insecure environment of unfaithfulness and selfishness. And, when people are insecure, they are easy prey for Satan to manipulate and control to do his dirty work of steal, kill and destroy.

Our acts of faithfulness and unselfishness are paramount to building trust. Our children are more sensitive to our behavior than we think. When we fail to do as promised; when we are slothful in the performance of promises, when we manipulate promises; we betray our family's trust and harm the integrity of our fatherhood. Whether it's a simple promise of carrying them to the shop, a vacation trip, or to purchase an item, we must do all within our power to be faithful. Naturally, there will be times when we will not be able to fulfill our promises. We are not God. However, even our failures can be a teaching lesson about our dependence on God.

Consistent unfaithfulness is a sign that a father is not focused. His energy and passion are devoted to himself, thus, he is unable to fulfill the will of God or the wishes of his family. He has not learned to prioritize. Remember God is first, and treating people with respect and love is a close second. When a father is faithful, he inspires his family to trust God and have confidence in having relationships with people. Most of all he leaves a legacy and roadmap for generations to come.

PROTECTOR

Akin to being faithful is being a protector through the wisdom of God. Many children's lives have been destroyed because a parent was unaware or unalert that a friend was influencing them to do wrong things. Or the child was being tempted with pornography or some other evil.

When a parent takes an active role in a child's life, it's not being over-protective; it's being proactive. An over-protective parent is a person suffering from insecurities and fear. As a result, they need the mastery of their children to feel secure. They never allow the person to be free to make their own choices. They, in their delusion, try to reincarnate themselves through their children.

The purpose of parenting is guidance; not domination and control. We want our children to learn and grow to be mature adults who are wise enough to make good and intelligent decisions for themselves. They shouldn't spend their lifetime trying to please "mommy" or "daddy."

In the early stages of our children lives, they are much too young to understand the prevailing evil and the many deceptions that assail them daily. They are ignorant of human behavior and how choices can impact a person's life not only for today but for a lifetime and even eternity. We must stand in the gap and protect them through prayer and proactive guidance.

We must watch the friends that they keep. This is the doorway that Satan usually uses to bring promiscuity, anger and lies. Do not be fooled by a smiling face! People wear masks and many parents, including me, have been tricked by children's friends that appeared very benign and innocent. But, behind closed doors they were the devil in disguise sent to seduce and destroy your child.

We must be alert to the things that they watch on TV and the internet. These are eye gates and ear gates to their souls and once they are bridged, Satan gains a foothold to manipulate and deceive them.

We must protect them from a school system that teaches things that are contrary to the word of God. Be alert to what is being taught in the classroom, the curriculum of the school, and who the teachers are. Attend the PTA meeting and be involved so that you can get a feel of the atmosphere where your child will be most of the time away from home.

TEACHER

"Seeing that Abraham shall surely become a great and mighty nation, and all the nations of the earth shall be blessed in him? For I know him, that he will command his children and his household after him, and they shall keep the way of the LORD, to do justice and judgment; that the LORD may bring upon Abraham that which he hath spoken of him." (Genesis 18:13-19)

"I will instruct thee and teach thee in the way which thou shalt go, I will guide thee with mine eye." (Psalm 32:8)

"Howbeit when he the Spirit of truth is come, he will guide you into all truth, for he shall not speak of himself; but whatsoever he shall hear that shall he speak and he will shew you things to come." (John 16:13)

"Study to shew thyself approved unto God, a workman that needeth not to be ashamed, rightly dividing the word of truth." (2 Timothy 2:15)

"And that from a child thou hast known the holy scriptures, which are able to make thee wise unto salvation through faith which is in Christ Jesus. All scripture is given by inspiration of God, and is profitable for doctrine, for reproof, for correction, for instruction in righteousness: That the man of God may be perfect, throughly furnished unto all good works." (2 Timothy 3:15-17)

A father must be a source and go to person for answers to life's constant and often perplexing questions. This doesn't mean a father needs to have all the answers, however, it does mean he should be a student of the Bible and an able or ready teacher. When a lot of people think about Bible teaching, they think it's about having a degree in theology, reading various Christian literature, and going to conferences and seminars. Whereas, the Lord does use all these avenues to educate His people, nothing can substitute for a personal and intimate relationship with the Lord. You must allow Him to teach and show you how truth is applied. Otherwise, the very truth that you are taught, and knowledge learned can handicap and drive you further from God.

As the above story shows, religiosity is the deadliest of the Devil's deceptions. When our hunger for knowledge supplants our desire for personal relationship with the Lord, we become form orientated. Getting the praise and accolades from people is more important than having compassion and being real and truthful. We become prideful and arrogant. This is the essence of the religious spirit that killed the Lord. The Scribes, Pharisees, and Sadducees were well educated about Jewish law, yet couldn't recognize the Creator when He stood right in front of them.

Since the inception of Christianity, we've never had this much access to Christian literature through books, tapes, CDs, magazine, movies, and the internet, yet revival lags and we are amidst a great apostasy. You see, God needs to reveal Himself to a man through circumstances, trials and experiences. This doesn't discount education; however, education must take a back seat to experience. The men who penned scriptures had a personal experience with God. Men like Moses, David, Samuel, Daniel, Peter and Paul experienced the truth behind the message and the reality of Father God.

Experience and knowledge must walk hand in hand. If the Holy Spirit moved men to write the scripture, then, the same Holy Spirit is needed to properly understand and apply scripture. This doesn't mean that we don't need the scriptures taught to us or we shouldn't take advantage of the many Bible helps such as concordances, and historical literature.

However, we do need a dependent relationship with the Holy Spirit who alone can give us the wisdom and understanding that we need. When a man turns daily from a life of selfishness and sin, his mind becomes clearer to the things of God.

Make time and properly prepare for Bible study and answering questions about the Bible. You can be innovative and make it a time of fun and reward for right answers given. Spend time with your wife studying the Bible together. Pick a passage of scripture and slowly go through looking for richer and deeper meaning. This gives you and your wife the opportunity to hear the inner voice of the Holy Spirit who can unlock the sometimes unclear meaning of scriptures. One of the most important things that you can teach your wife and children is to be sensitive to the voice of the Holy Spirit. These times of study and prayer will substantiate the scriptures as the foundation of truth for your family.

In this same vein, let your greatest teaching tool be the example of godly behavior that you exhibit daily before your family. *"Neither as being lords over God's heritage, but being ensamples to the flock." (1Peter 5:3)* Genuine and consistent piety verifies that God lives within your heart and you are not just another religious fake. Many family members have been disappointed when they found out that Dad was nothing more than a hypocrite who hid behind a charade of church activity and Bible pounding. We want to live better and more real lives than the Scribes and Pharisees. Who were the Scribes and Pharisees? They were nothing more than educated religious bigots who used their religion for their own selfish prideful glory and fame. They were never really interested in bringing healing or directing people to the True and Living God. To them, religion was money, recognition and control.

The spirit of religiosity is rooted in pride. It deceives us from humbling ourselves and seeking God. Instead, our goals are very earthly. We want people to worship us instead of seeking and worshiping the Lord. This spirit also makes us independent and insensitive. As a result, we teach and groom our children to pursue the rainbow of success. Whereas, we should always teach our children to be hard workers and excellent in all that they do, the greatest success in life is not money or fame; it's having a close relationship with the Lord. Things and success can't give you peace and true security in life. *"And he said unto them, Take heed, and beware of covetousness: for a man's life consisteth not in the abundance of the things which he possesseth." (Luke12:15)*

What we teach our children should always be God-centered. We don't want them to be religious…we want them to be real. Actions always speak louder than words and show is always better than tell. So, what we teach should always be backed up with concrete actions of love and kindness.

DISCIPLINARIAN

"FOOLISHNESS IS BOUND IN THE HEART OF A CHILD; BUT THE ROD OF CORRECTION SHALL DRIVE IT FAR FROM HIM." (PROVERBS 22:15)

"HE THAT SPARETH HIS ROD HATETH HIS SON; BUT HE THAT LOVETH HIM CHASTENETH HIM BETIMES." (PROVERBS 12:24)

"AND YE HAVE FORGOTTEN THE EXHORTATION WHICH SPEAKETH UNTO YOU AS UNTO CHILDREN, MY SON, DESPISE NOT THOU THE CHASTENING OF THE LORD, NOR FAINT WHEN THOU ART REBUKED OF HIM. FOR WHO THE LORD LOVETH HE CHASTENETH, AND SCOURETH EVERY SON WHOM HE RECEIVETH. IF YE ENDURE CHASTENING, GOD DEALETH WITH YOU AS WITH SONS; FOR WHAT SON IS HE WHOM THE FATHER CHASTENETH NOT: BUT IF YE BE WITHOUT CHASTISEMENT, WHEREOF ALL ARE PARTAKERS, THEN ARE YE BASTARDS, AND NOT SONS. FURTHERMORE, WE HAVE HAD FATHERS OF OUR FLESH WHICH CORRECTED US, AND WE GAVE THEM REVERENCE; SHALL WE NOT MUCH RATHER BE IN SUBJECTION UNTO THE FATHER OF SPIRITS AND LIVE: FOR THEY VERILY FOR A FEW DAYS CHASTENED US AFTER THEIR OWN PLEASURE; BUT HE FOR OUR PROFIT THAT WE MIGHT BE PARTAKER OF HIS HOLINESS.NOW NO CHASTENING FOR THE PRESENT SEEMETH

TO BE JOYOUS, BUT GRIEVOUS NEVERTHELESS AFTERWARD IT YIELDETH THE PEACEABLE FRUIT OF RIGHTEOUSNESS UNTO THEM WHICH ARE EXERCISED THEREBY." (HEBREWS 12:5-11)

"AND, YE FATHERS, PROVOKE NOT YOUR CHILDREN TO WRATH: BUT BRING THEM UP IN THE NURTURE AND ADMONITION OF THE LORD." (EPHESIANS 6:4)

"A BISHOP THEN MUST BE BLAMELESS, THE HUSBAND OF ONE WIFE, VIGILANT, SOBER, OF GOOD BEHAVIOUR, GIVEN TO HOSPITALITY, APT TO TEACH; NOT GIVEN TO WINE, NO STRIKER, NOT GREEDY OF FILTHY LUCRE; BUT PATIENT, NOT A BRAWLER, NOT COVETOUS; ONE THAT RULETH WELL HIS OWN HOUSE, HAVING HIS CHILDREN IN SUBJECTION WITH ALL GRAVITY." (1 TIMOTHY 3:2-4)

Discipline is a very important aspect of being a father and should never be neglected. Whether it comes in the form of: rebuke, scolding, corporal punishment or a simple reprimand, discipline is the way of molding a child's will in the right direction. When we love people, we don't see them doing something wrong or detrimental and do nothing about it. If we do nothing now, the slothful behavior turns into foolish excuses; the insensitive attitude turns into self-centeredness; and the disrespectful attitude will turn into hardened rebellion against authority later in life. The undisciplined behavior becomes a problem to the teacher in the classroom and eventual work for the police officer in the community. Like the Bible says, *"The rod and reproof give wisdom: but a child left to himself bringeth his mother to shame." (Proverbs 29:15)*

Discipline teaches a child to be self-aware and responsible for his actions. He learns through discipline respect for others and his environment. He also learns that bad behavior brings penalties and punishment. This mindset must be engrained in a child's psyche in order for him to be a mature adult. Without a conscience of right and wrong or sensitivity to others, a person will eventually become a hazard and burden to society. He may struggle to keep a job because he is consistently late or absent because of lack of focus or simply being lazy. Or, his insensitivity to others makes him brutal and crude in his behavior.

During our modern times, there have been psychologists who have been against corporal punishment such as spanking or using a belt to discipline. They claim that it's barbaric, draconian, and abusive. They advise us to use less abrasive methods like 'timeouts' and taking away privileges. Whereas, a father should never discipline a child with out-of-control anger, corporal punishment like spanking and using the belt or paddle are legitimate forms of punishment if used under control and temperately. God's word is truth…let me say that again for impact…God's word is truth.

Those of us who have been beaten with belts, tree limbs, and hangers know that it works, when it is done with love and care. It may sound cruel or inhumane, however, when a father acts in love to discipline his child, he is not beating out of brutality to abuse his child. His aim is not to maim. His aim is to exact punishment to tame the will and direct it in another direction. The driving force is not hate, it's love and a desire for education and healing. When love is the foundation, the beating is tempered and always under control. It's not done viciously and with malice. It is carefully pre-planned, calibrated and stopped.

However, when we do decide to discipline whether it's a minor infraction like forgetting to clean up after oneself or something more serious such as disrespect for authority, a plan must always be in place about what discipline is appropriate. Whether it's as simple as taking away privileges, a soft reprimand or corporal punishment where a paddle or belt is used, we must always be in control. There are times when what is done leads to anger, but we must temper our anger with good judgment. If you can't balance your anger with good judgment, meaning the appropriate discipline meets the infraction, then, discipline should be put off until later.

Never should a child be disciplined by an out-of-control parent who has lost sound judgment. This can lead to abuse and the reason you should always have a discipline plan in place that is meticulously followed. Love should always be the motivating factor and not what the neighbors or society think. Some parents take harsh and punitive actions or take no action at all based on what others may say or think about them.

I remember a pastor whose daughter became pregnant. Of course, this was a great embarrassment to his ministry. However, instead of trying to restore his suffering and emotionally distraught daughter, he threw her out the house after being scorned by church members and other pastors. His daughter later moved into an apartment with her baby's father. The pastor thought he was doing the right thing. His daughter was having premarital sex and he was right for making an example out of her.

Of course, this was pure ignorance and another example of the religious spirit that shows no mercy. Our children do need discipline when they have done wrong. However, our discipline should never be the result of our pride: what will people think about me! Personally, as a sensitive father, he should have been more aware of the enemy's attack against his daughter. Then, after it was brought out into the open, he should have embraced and covered his daughter's shame. That's when she really really (purposely repeated) needed him. When our children are down and out, they don't need an executioner and judge. They need a father who forgives, restores and provides healing. The fruit of discipline should never be a bruised spirit. The fruit of discipline should be healing and resolve to do better.

THERE IS POWER IN WHAT YOU SAY

"DEATH AND LIFE ARE IN THE POWER OF THE TONGUE AND THEY THAT LOVE IT SHALL EAT THE FRUIT THEREOF." (PROVERBS 18:21)

"HE THAT HATH KNOWLEDGE SPARETH HIS WORDS AND A MAN OF UNDERSTANDING IS OF AN EXCELLENT SPIRIT." (PROVERBS 17:27-28)

"LET YOUR SPEECH BE ALWAYS WITH GRACE, SEASONED WITH SALT, THAT YE MAY KNOW HOW YE OUGHT TO ANSWER EVERY MAN." (COLOSSIAN 4:6)

"FOR VERILY I SAY UNTO YOU, THAT WHOSOEVER SHALL SAY
UNTO THIS MOUNTAIN, BE THOU REMOVED AND BE THOU CAST
INTO THE SEA; AND SHALL NOT DOUBT IN HIS HEART, BUT
SHALL BELIEVE THAT THOSE THINGS WHICH HE SAITH SHALL
COME TO PASS; HE SHALL HAVE WHATSOEVER HE SAITH."
(MARK 11:23)

Most people are unaware of how powerful their words are. Words emanate from within our hearts and influence our environment for good or bad. Words can build and encourage, they can also bruise, destroy and discourage. The Bible constantly implores us to use our words sparingly and with much wisdom.

This indeed takes time and training, but we must tame our tongues. If we don't, we risk hurting the people around us and negatively impacting their destiny. Calling someone a derogatory name or constantly bringing up mistakes and thrusting them into the face of a child are counter-productive. When we do this, we make the mountains harder to climb and the valleys too steep to mount.

Words are thoughts and feelings and when they are uttered they represent a world that someone must live in. If we are the authority and we are constantly saying negative things about our children, how can they have a positive self-esteem? How can they have faith to face a world that is full of challenges? We destroy the fruit before it has time to ripen.

Furthermore, as fathers, because words are so powerful, we can actually shape a person's destiny by speaking either positive or negative things over their life. If we are their source and mentor why wouldn't they believe us? Why wouldn't they trust our judgment? We also open spiritual doors in our children's lives by speaking blessings or curses over their lives. Indeed, some of the most destructive behavior we see in the world today is because of a father speaking negative words over a child. Contra wise some of the most innovative and brightest minds were nourished by a parent who prophesied hope and faith into their child.

Throughout the Old Testament, it was the culture of the father to bless the children especially while they were passing away. Fathers represent the gateway to the future because he is the authority, source and mentor of his generations and posterity. Indeed, what we see in the world today is a direct result of men and fathers refusing to embrace godly authority to keep righteous seed on the earth. Be a blessing to your generations by humbling yourself before the Lord and being full of compassion, faithful, a teacher, disciplinarian, and one who speaks blessing that your children so desperately need.

CHAPTER 9

THE MATURE MAN

During my teenage years, I went to the movies to watch a lot of James Bond, Western and Kung Fu movies. Men in these movies were very confident, got the girl, and overcame their adversaries. Movies are still produced with this type of story line, however, during that time I believe it was the culture. Back then, men were still the head of the home and the prime providers. That has changed drastically.

Most men today are passive, divorced, earning less than their wives and confused about their identity. As women gained more leverage in the world and divorce vacated the male position in the home, young men, particularly, have struggled to understand who they are and what is their role in the world.

The devil fooled men then, and he is fooling men now. It's not what the movies projected. It was never about pride. It's not what you think about yourself or circumstances. It's not what the president, a political party or the media says is the truth about being a man. And yes, mankind is equal. The genders are equal, however, and as always, God is a God of purpose and order. He is the manufacturer and decides how His product should be used. You can never reach your goal of maturity listening to lies spawned in the crevasses of hell. God's word is truth. Like one Psalmist said, *"Blessed is the man that walketh not in the counsel of the ungodly, nor standeth in the way of sinners, nor sitteth in the seat of the scornful. But his delight is in the law of the LORD; and in his law doth he meditate day and night." (Psalm 1:1-2)*

Understanding what male maturity is, and getting there has always been the dilemma. We, men, lack the faith, patience and most of all the humility to let go and let God. We still believe the corrupt adage that says, *"God only helps those who help themselves."* It sounds legitimate and honorable but it's far from the truth. God only helps those who have filed for human bankruptcy and admit that they are poor, needy, and unable to help themselves. He only listens to those who walk in faith and belief in His unlimited power. Like David said, *"This poor man cried, and the LORD heard him, and saved him out of all his troubles." (Psalm 34:6)* God has to do this!

The arrogant male protagonists in the movies of yesteryear were always a delusion. Charismatic, self-willed and self-motivated looks attractive but it's a lie that indulges your pride and puts you on the wrong road to failure and shame. When you make yourself God and refuse to listen to the voice of wisdom, you isolate yourself from help. God is always talking and willing to help us, our problem is pride and an obstinate refusal to listen.

Most movies revolved around revenge and scripts showcasing the so-called "triumph of the human spirit." These scripts, written by unsaved people who have very limited knowledge about the Creator, can only lead us further from the truth and what it means to be a real and mature man. In fact, and as always, truth is opposite to what the world proclaims and puts forward.

GOD'S LEADER

"AND THOU SHALT LOVE THE LORD THY GOD WITH ALL THY HEART, AND WITH ALL THY SOUL, AND WITH ALL THY MIND, AND WITH ALL THY STRENGTH: THIS IS THE FIRST COMMANDMENT. AND THE SECOND IS LIKE, NAMELY THIS,

THOU SHALT LOVE THY NEIGHBOUR AS THYSELF. THERE
IS NONE OTHER COMMANDMENT GREATER THAN THESE."
(MARK 12:30-31)

"AND SAMUEL SAID, HATH THE LORD AS GREAT DELIGHT IN
BURNT OFFERINGS AND SACRIFICES, AS IN OBEYING THE VOICE
OF THE LORD? BEHOLD, TO OBEY IS BETTER THAN SACRIFICE,
AND TO HEARKEN THAN THE FAT OF RAMS." (1 SAMUEL 15:22)

"LET THIS MIND BE IN YOU, WHICH WAS ALSO IN CHRIST
JESUS: WHO, BEING IN THE FORM OF GOD, THOUGHT IT NOT
ROBBERY TO BE EQUAL WITH GOD: BUT MADE HIMSELF OF NO
REPUTATION, AND TOOK UPON HIM THE FORM OF A SERVANT,
AND WAS MADE IN THE LIKENESS OF MEN: AND BEING FOUND
IN FASHION AS A MAN, HE HUMBLED HIMSELF, AND BECAME
OBEDIENT UNTO DEATH, EVEN THE DEATH OF THE CROSS.
WHEREFORE GOD ALSO HATH HIGHLY EXALTED HIM, AND
GIVEN HIM A NAME WHICH IS ABOVE EVERY NAME: THAT AT
THE NAME OF JESUS EVERY KNEE SHOULD BOW, OF THINGS
IN HEAVEN, AND THINGS IN EARTH, AND THINGS UNDER THE
EARTH; AND THAT EVERY TONGUE SHOULD CONFESS THAT
JESUS CHRIST IS LORD, TO THE GLORY OF GOD THE FATHER."
(PHILIPPIANS 2:5-11)

Saul, the first king of Israel, was rejected by the Lord because of his disobedience. When God gave him a commandment to destroy the Amalekites, and everything in their cities, he saved the King of the Amalekites from death, and saved some of the choice goats and sheep. He disobeyed the command of the Lord which shows that he was a god to himself. He did what he felt was right even though he was commanded differently. He was not a focused leader.

He was a poor leader whose disobedience would have influenced the whole nation to disrespect the word of God. Loving God and obeying his word should be the focus of a leader. Our obedience and submission to God is our demonstration of love. Every leader who was successful in the Bible did this. Abraham, Moses, Joshua, and David, to name a few, are men that demonstrated their love for the Lord, by obeying His word. Loving God and obeying His commandment is the whole duty of man. That is your number one focus in life.

Adam, the first man, failed because he neglected this. God told Adam not to eat the fruit of Good and Evil. It was his test. Would he demonstrate his love to God by being obedient or would he disobey and show himself to be selfish or a lover of self? As you know, Adam did the latter. He lost focus. He was blinded by the lie that he didn't need the Lord and he could be a god himself.

Submission, yes submission, a word that men like to attribute to their wives and everyone else, is the key to the Lord's favor and His loving kindness. It's proof of our love. Whether it's a command to do something or simply yielding to the Lord in the tribulations and the trials He allows into our lives, when we submit, we invite and garner His favor.

When we are stubborn and act independent to the word of God, when we complain when He allows trials into our lives, we set ourselves up for failure. The message that we are speaking loud and clear is, "We don't need you, Lord, and can do it all by ourselves." Or, "I don't deserve what you are allowing in my life." Theses faithless attitudes ostracize us from the grace and wisdom of God.

Jesus said, *"He that hath my commandments, and keepeth them, he it is that loveth me: and he that loveth me shall be loved of my Father, and I will love him, and will manifest myself to him." (John 14:21)* Without God's wisdom and guidance, we are fodder for the enemy, Satan, who is created on a higher level than us, has spiritual tools and powers in his arsenal to deceive and manipulate us. So, to be a great leader requires being diligent and attentive to the things that the Lord tells us, whether it's the revelation in His word, the wise words of a wife, friend, co-worker or the voice of our children. Be focused.

One of the greatest leaders in the Bible, other than our Lord was David the son of Jesse. God called him a man after His own heart; in other words, he acts like Me. So, what made David a man after God's heart?

David was a military man who killed a lot of people. He also committed adultery and murdered the husband of the woman with whom he had the affair. How could he be a man after God's own heart? How?

What set David apart? Genuineness and sensitivity. David made mistakes, however, when he was rebuked and corrected, he yielded. He didn't try to defend himself. Most people, who are in a position of authority, would try to destroy the person who would dare to tell them that they were wrong. When the Prophet Nathan rebuked David for his adulterous behavior, and subsequent killing of Uriah the Hittite, the woman's husband, he was sorry and repented. He embraced the truth. Psalm 51, a song of repentance, was a result of that encounter.

This showed that David was a very genuine and sincere person. None of us are good. None! However, if we truly humble ourselves before God, He can grace us with His wisdom and goodness. David displayed a genuine and sincere attitude.

King David also had a very sensitive heart. And, if we truly have a relationship with the Lord, He teaches us and makes us sensitive to His creation. He teaches us to care for people and to be unselfish, because that's His heart. Love also makes us transparent and very real! Let me repeat that: love makes us transparent and very real! David was genuine and very sensitive! David was merciful even to his enemies. Yes, he made mistakes, but he was willing to admit them. He cared about other people and even treated his enemies with kindness. His love for God and care for the people of Israel was his motivation in battle. He was a very focused individual who was on a mission to fulfill God's purpose for his life. Yes, God is like that, *"But I say unto you, Love your enemies, bless them that curse you, do good to them that hate you, and pray for them which despitefully use you, and persecute you; That ye may be the children of your Father which is in heaven: for he maketh his sun to rise on the evil and on the good, and sendeth rain on the just and on the unjust."* *(Matthew 5:44-45)* Perfect in this sense means mature and genuine; not holding grudges, not being two-faced and being gracious and kind to others. Immaturity always shows itself as a selfish and self-centered individual whose only interest is looking out for number one.

David formed an unbreakable bond with Johnathan the son of Saul. Their friendship was said to be above that of a man's love for a woman. No, they weren't homosexuals! They were completely transparent with each other and always considered each other's needs. Wow! We all want to have friends like that; friends who not only have our backs but are genuine, truthful and real. This is the way marriage should be, but in most cases, because of selfishness, most husband and wives don't know how to be a true friend.

Nothing hurts friendships like the breaking of trust and instability. When we are more interested in getting accolades and the praise of people; when we are controlled by pride rather than receiving God's pleasure, we can't be trustworthy. Our hearts are tainted, corrupted and twisted. Our focus is self.

This was the big difference between Saul who was rejected by the Lord and David. Their focus was different. One was more interested in pleasing God and doing His will and the other was focused on what people thought about him and doing things independently from the voice of the Lord.

ENDURING PERSECUTION, TRIALS AND TEMPTATION

"THESE THINGS I HAVE SPOKEN UNTO YOU, THAT IN ME YE MIGHT HAVE PEACE. IN THE WORLD YE SHALL HAVE TRIBULATION: BUT BE OF GOOD CHEER; I HAVE OVERCOME THE WORLD." (JOHN 16:33)

"BLESSED ARE YE, WHEN MEN SHALL REVILE YOU, AND PERSECUTE YOU, AND SHALL SAY ALL MANNER OF EVIL AGAINST YOU FALSELY, FOR MY SAKE." (MATTHEW 5:11)

"YE ADULTERERS AND ADULTERESSES, KNOW YE NOT THAT THE FRIENDSHIP OF THE WORLD IS ENMITY WITH GOD?

WHOSOEVER THEREFORE WILL BE A FRIEND OF THE WORLD IS THE ENEMY OF GOD." (JAMES 4:4)

"AND WE KNOW THAT ALL THINGS WORK TOGETHER FOR GOOD TO THEM THAT LOVE GOD, TO THEM WHO ARE THE CALLED ACCORDING TO HIS PURPOSE." (ROMANS 8:28)

"FOR THIS THING I BESOUGHT THE LORD THRICE, THAT IT MIGHT DEPART FROM ME. AND HE SAID UNTO ME, MY GRACE IS SUFFICIENT FOR THEE: FOR MY STRENGTH IS MADE PERFECT IN WEAKNESS. MOST GLADLY THEREFORE WILL I RATHER GLORY IN MY INFIRMITIES, THAT THE POWER OF CHRIST MAY REST UPON ME. THEREFORE I TAKE PLEASURE IN INFIRMITIES, IN REPROACHES, IN NECESSITIES, IN PERSECUTIONS, IN DISTRESSES FOR CHRIST'S SAKE: FOR WHEN I AM WEAK, THEN AM I STRONG." (2 CORINTHIANS 12:3-10)

Tribulation or trials are a part of the human experience. They can't be avoided. However, we have a choice. We can go through tribulations without God's grace or we can bring Him on board and allow Him to be our strength and help when we go through difficult times. These storms of life are not meant to devastate or destroy us, rather they are meant to build character through faith and patience. Every persecution, trial or temptation is a teaching lesson that God is always in control. They are also lessons on brokenness and our utter dependency on the Lord.

Few people, few indeed are able to endure these storms that seem to "pop up" from nowhere. It was not your fault, yet a relative or friend falsely accuses you; business or personal financial failure and lack; unfair persecution in the community, on your job or at home; sexual temptation; marital problems; a child rebelling and the list can go on.

We must remember that these have been allowed for us to experience His grace and wisdom; and to learn never to depend on self. Never depend on self! In fact, when we humble ourselves in the midst of our trials and offer them up to the Lord in faith, He gives us more grace; grace to experience His wisdom, glory and miraculous power. Wow! The Apostle

Paul reached a place in his life where he embraced his trials so that he can experience more of God's loving favor and kindness…just resting on Him!

Storms come when you least expect them and at the most inopportune times. Most people, like the Israelites in the wilderness grow bitter and complain. We miss the opportunity to become patient; the very essence of maturity. Like a songwriter penned, "I care not today what tomorrow may bring sunshine, sorrow or rain. The Lord I know rule over everything and all of my worry is vain. Yes, I'm living by faith in Jesus above." Life is not a sprint race, it's a marathon. You must run this race with patience.

Many acts of persecution are recorded in the gospels and in the Acts of the Apostles. (the true name should be Acts of the Holy Spirit) No one likes to be singled out as the odd one. However, when we serve the Lord, we become odd to the people of this world. In fact, many of them hate Christian people. We think differently. Our lives revolve around the things of God, contra wise the lives of people who don't follow the Lord revolve around money, flesh and self-worship. Their master and lord is the evil one who hates light and understanding.

People persecute because the light of our lives reveal the darkness in their lives. So, their constant aim is to diminish the light. They want to accuse; abuse; to lie on; to defraud Christians in an attempt to disprove the truth that we have. However, as it was in the early church, persecution only makes the light burn more brightly. You can never fight God and win. Never! God will always have the last say. When the Pharisees killed the Lord, He arose from the dead and sent the Holy Spirit to empower the church. Miracles, signs and wonders were abundant, and the church grew by leaps and bounds.

You see, whether it's a tribulation, trial or persecution, God allows it to grow us. It's a blessing in disguise! They remove layer by layer the imperfections from us. Our insecurities and fears are attitudes of deception that keep us from seeing the Lord…really seeing Him! And, when our storms, trials and persecution come, we learn that only He can help us. We grow in faith as we discard our garments of pride and self-effort.

PATIENCE: THE EPITOME OF MATURITY

"Wait I say on the Lord; be of good courage, and he shall strengthen thine heart: wait, I say on the Lord." (Psalm 27:14)

"They that wait on the Lord, shall renew their strength. They shall mount up with wings as eagles. They shall run and not be weary. Walk and not faint." (Isaiah 40:31)

"My brethren, count it all joy when ye fall into divers temptations; Knowing this, that the trying of your faith worketh patience. But let patience have her perfect work, that ye may be perfect and entire, wanting nothing." (James 1:2-4)

"In your patience possess ye your souls." (Luke 21:19)

"Take, my brethren, the prophets, who have spoken in the name of the Lord, for an example of suffering affliction, and of patience. Behold, we count them happy which endure. Ye have heard of the patience of Job, and have seen the end of the Lord; that the Lord is very pitiful, and of tender mercy." (James 5:10-11)

"Wherefore seeing we also are compassed about with so great a cloud of witnesses, let us lay aside every weight, and the sin which doth so easily beset us, and let us run with patience the race that is set before us." (Hebrews 12:1)

Most people can at least stay patient for a little while during a very trying time, as they wait for the Lord to change and give them victory in their circumstances. But, true and genuine faith is the sacrifice of worship and praise…even if the circumstances don't change. You see, genuine faith is not in what God does, it's faith in who He is. Do you really know the Lord? Do you? These are the people who can survive no matter what the circumstances around them are. Whether it's lack, sickness, rejection from family and friends, these golden faith people thrive because they know Him.

Even a man of faith and power like Elijah lacked wisdom in this area. He had faced the four hundred prophets of Baal and called down fire from heaven, yet, he ran and fell into depression when Jezebel threatened to kill him after perhaps one of the greatest miracles in history-fire falling from the sky and consuming water and sacrifice. He couldn't wait. He wanted things in Israel to go back to normal after the people had showed repentance.

But, a deeper knowledge of God would have revealed to him the perfect plan of God. After forty days of fasting and prayer he finally got it. God was not in the powerful wind; God was not in the fire; God was not in the earthquake. Yes, He is a God of miracles. These are all things that God does! God is a person of relationship. He is love. Patience teaches us never to judge after what we see but to judge righteously and by what He shows us in our hearts.

Patient people are compassionate and forgive because they know that it's God's grace that makes the difference between human and human. Patient people are temperate because they can overlook the faults of others knowing that everyone fails. Like Job who said, "My righteousness I hold fast and wont' let it go," patient people are determined to wait because they truly believe in the Lord! Patient people are unperturbed by circumstances because they know that God is in total and complete control. Always!

Without patience, time becomes an enemy instead of an ally. We complain. We make foolish choices. For example, the man or woman who marries just to have sex rather than waiting for character to reveal itself and God to provide a compatible mate. There are people who would rather borrow money than live within their means and wait on God's provision.

When Job's wife told him to curse God and die in the midst of his anguish and pain, he refused. He was determined to wait on the Lord! He couldn't understand the reason for his suffering but his experience with the Lord told him to be patient and trust…God would bring him out! Like someone said, "He may not come when you want Him…but He will always be on time!"

THE WISDOM OF WORDS

"LET YOUR SPEECH BE ALWAYS WITH GRACE, SEASONED WITH SALT, THAT YE MAY KNOW HOW YE OUGHT TO ANSWER EVERY MAN." (COLOSSIANS 4:6)

"IF ANY MAN SPEAK, LET HIM SPEAK AS THE ORACLES OF GOD; IF ANY MAN MINISTER, LET HIM DO IT AS OF THE ABILITY WHICH GOD GIVETH: THAT GOD IN ALL THINGS MAY BE GLORIFIED THROUGH JESUS CHRIST, TO WHOM BE PRAISE AND DOMINION FOR EVER AND EVER. AMEN." (1 PETER 4:11)

"BUT LET IT BE THE HIDDEN MAN OF THE HEART, IN THAT WHICH IS NOT CORRUPTIBLE, EVEN THE ORNAMENT OF A MEEK AND QUIET SPIRIT, WHICH IS IN THE SIGHT OF GOD OF GREAT PRICE." (1 PETER 3:4)

"EVEN A FOOL, WHEN HE HOLDETH HIS PEACE, IS COUNTED WISE: AND HE THAT SHUTTETH HIS LIPS IS ESTEEMED A MAN OF UNDERSTANDING." (PROVERBS 17:28)

"AND THAT YE STUDY TO BE QUIET, AND TO DO YOUR OWN BUSINESS, AND TO WORK WITH YOUR OWN HANDS, AS WE COMMANDED YOU." (1 THESSALONIANS 4:11)

"HE THAT HATH KNOWLEDGE SPARETH HIS WORDS: AND A MAN OF UNDERSTANDING IS OF AN EXCELLENT SPIRIT." (PROVERBS 17:27)

"WHOSO KEEPETH HIS MOUTH AND HIS TONGUE KEEPETH HIS SOUL FROM TROUBLES." (PROVERBS 21:23)

"A GOOD MAN OUT OF THE GOOD TREASURE OF HIS HEART BRINGETH FORTH THAT WHICH IS GOOD; AND AN EVIL MAN OUT OF THE EVIL TREASURE OF HIS HEART BRINGETH FORTH THAT WHICH IS EVIL: FOR OF THE ABUNDANCE OF THE HEART HIS MOUTH SPEAKETH." (LUKE 6:45)

"NEITHER FILTHINESS, NOR FOOLISH TALKING, NOR JESTING, WHICH ARE NOT CONVENIENT: BUT RATHER GIVING OF THANKS." (EPHESIANS 5:4)

"IN THE MULTITUDE OF WORDS THERE WANTETH NOT SIN: BUT HE THAT REFRAINETH HIS LIPS IS WISE." (PROVERBS 10:10)

One of my greatest mistakes as a young believer was talking too much. I had a lot of information and I wanted to let people know that "I knew." I was well-read, I had received some revelation from the Lord and I needed to speak. However, many times my judgment on the "when" was poor. Sometimes I was at work on my employer's time. Or, I met someone and felt a need to let them know "how things work" spiritually. But, even though what I was saying was true, it was not the right time. I was ahead of the Lord or I was revealing information to someone who was not qualified or eligible to receive it.

The tongue is difficult to tame, however, digging deeper, it's really our hearts that need clearance and healing. Scripture says out of the abundance of the heart doth the mouth speak, and, *keep thine heart with all diligence for out of it are the issue of life.* When our mouths are contrary and disobedient, we must check our hearts. Most of the time it's unbroken pride and the need to be noticed or better worshipped. We need to be seen as having intellectual clout or we need to subdue another with our wealth of knowledge and wisdom.

Other times, it's issues we haven't deal with; past hurts and wounds that were buried and get aggravated when a particular subject is brought up.

Like an open wound and sore, it's a very tender spot. Some people get very belligerent and argumentative when they feel that their issue has been raised and brought to the forefront. They feel a need to defend themselves-from most of the time an illusionary foe.

As foresaid, my religious knowledge was my talking points and although what I was saying was the truth, I neglected the Lord's timing. So, I was speaking head knowledge and not what the Lord really wanted me to say. He knows the heart of people and He knows whether they are ready for the precious truth that will be revealed to them. We must wait on Him for words of wisdom that are timely and potent; words that bring light, revelation and most of all deliverance from the deceptions of Satan.

For us to embrace this level of maturity, we must study...really study to be quiet! Sometimes I kick myself when I realize too much is being said. We must rein in our thoughts even the good ones so that the Holy Spirit can be the master of our words. That's the reason even jesting or "the making of jokes" is a distraction and very counter-productive to spiritual growth in us and in others. Although laughter and wit have their place, especially when making a good point, they should be used sparingly as they can negate the point that we are always living in the presence of a holy God.

The ability to tame the tongue is the essence of spiritual maturity and was demonstrated by our Lord when He was arrested and being questioned by Pontius Pilate. The Bible said that at one point that Jesus was simply quiet. He had an opportunity to defend Himself-like most of us like to do to show our innocence or intelligence-instead He left everything in God's hands. He was broken and mature.

PATHWAY TO DOMINION

"BUT SEEK YE FIRST THE KINGDOM OF GOD, AND HIS RIGHTEOUSNESS; AND ALL THESE THINGS SHALL BE ADDED UNTO YOU. TAKE THEREFORE NO THOUGHT FOR THE MORROW: FOR THE MORROW SHALL TAKE THOUGHT FOR THE THINGS

OF ITSELF. SUFFICIENT UNTO THE DAY IS THE EVIL THEREOF."
(MATTHEW 6:33-34)

"AND GOD BLESSED THEM, AND GOD SAID UNTO THEM, BE
FRUITFUL, AND MULTIPLY, AND REPLENISH THE EARTH, AND
SUBDUE IT: AND HAVE DOMINION OVER THE FISH OF THE SEA,
AND OVER THE FOWL OF THE AIR, AND OVER EVERY LIVING
THING THAT MOVETH UPON THE EARTH." (GENESIS 1:28)

"FOR AS MANY AS ARE LED BY THE SPIRIT OF GOD, THY ARE
THE SONS OF GOD." (ROMANS 8:14)

"BEHOLD I GIVE UNTO YOU POWER TO TREAD ON SERPENTS
AND SCORPIONS, AND OVER ALL THE POWER OF THE ENEMY:
AND NOTHING SHALL BY ANY MEANS HURT YOU." (LUKE 10:19)
"AND IT SHALL COME TO PASS, IF THOU SHALT HEARKEN
DILIGENTLY UNTO; THE VOICE OF THE LORD THY GOD, TO
OBSERVE AND TO DO ALL HIS COMMANDMENTS WHICH I
COMMAND THEE THIS DAY, THAT THE LORD THY GOD WILL
SET THEE ON HIGH ABOVE ALL NATIONS OF THE EARTH: AND
ALL THESE BLESSINGS SHALL COME ON THEE, AND OVERTAKE
THEE, IF THOU SHALT HEARKEN UNTO THE VOICE OF THE
LORD THY GOD." (DEUTERONOMY 28:1-2)

When God gave man the authority in the garden, He gave him the
authority to have dominion. Dominion is translated from a Hebrew
word "radah" and means: to tread down, subjugate, to crumble, to prevail
against, to reign, and to rule. Man was commissioned by God as being the
ruler and custodian over the earth. He was not just a mouthpiece saying
that he was in control. Man was the god of this world. However, in the
mechanics of his dominion, we must always remember the Holy Spirit.

Man's dominion was exhibited as he allowed the Holy Spirit to influence
his actions and behavior. Adam would ensure that his garden tasks were
accomplished before his scheduled meeting with God. He knew exactly
what to name the animals. He knew how to talk and communicate with
God. He knew what to name his wife. This was dominion.

Adam walked in complete faith and trust in God and his sinless nature was a riverbed for the flow of God's wisdom. But when Adam sinned, rebellion clogged up his spiritual arteries. Instead of operating in the depth of God's wisdom, he could use only ten percent of his brain. True story! He had to call on God to come and fill the void that was in his life. But it was never like it was before.

Although men of God like Solomon, Daniel and David demonstrated the wisdom of God, man's full restoration came when Jesus Christ went to Calvary and restored dominion back to man through His blood. God could reconnect with the spirit of man, forming a new man created in the image and likeness of God. *"Therefore if any man be in Christ, he is a new creature: old things are passed away; behold, all things are become new."* *(2 Corinthians 5:17)* Now, with Jesus Christ living within us, we have all the tools necessary to operate in dominion; the way God designed man to operate.

However, although man's spirit nature is reborn, he still lives in a fleshly body and his mind or soul needs renewal. Renewal comes as a man daily submits to the Holy Spirit who energizes the new man. That is why the Devil fights to confuse and obliterate the doctrines of the Blood of Jesus Christ, the Baptism of the Holy Spirit and walking in the Spirit. He knows that these doctrines are fundamental to achieving dominion. *"Howbeit when he, the Spirit of truth, is come, he will guide you into all truth, for he shall not speak of himself, but whatsoever he shall hear, that shall he speak: and he will shew you things to come."* *(John 16:13)* *"But ye shall receive power, after that the Holy Ghost is come upon you: and ye shall be witnesses unto me both in Jerusalem, and in all Judaea, and in Samaria, and unto the uttermost part of the earth."* *(Acts 1:8)*

When a person is renewed through the blood of Jesus Christ and the power of the Holy Spirit, they have been given dominion. They have been given authority to dominate every area of their lives. For a man, God expects him to control his position as head of the home. God doesn't want him to be a mediocre protector, God wants him to beat the devil up and kick him out of the family! God wants to make him a father of excellence and integrity. God wants to make him an able teacher by revealing divine secrets to him. God does not want him to be a lackadaisical provider; God wants him to be a man proficient with finances.

In most households, just the opposite is true. The average family is growing in debt. The devil is beating up men and kicking them out of their own homes. Children have become oppressors, and love life between husband and wife stinks! But I say to every man who is reading this book, your wife's happiness, your financial abundance, your children's salvation, are all wrapped up in you, and your authority in the home. You must exercise dominion by submitting yourself to the power of the Holy Spirit and faith in the finished work at Calvary.

Now I am going to give you a key that will unlock God's blessing upon your life. Faith. Wait a minute, you say, I have read about faith and I have practiced faith. I have preached faith. But I guarantee you, if you look back, in most cases, it was misguided faith; faith that was based on your own fleshly desires and expectations; the faith that most charismatic circles preach. Faith that causes people to be presumptuous and self-centered, believing that God is going to give them their every fleshly desire and bless their carnal decisions. God is not a genie. He is Lord and King, and we are His servants. He is the shepherd and we are the sheep. Yes, He has promised to meet our needs and "bless our socks off," but the promises are always conditional upon our obedience.

God does not revolve around our needs and fancies. As we obey, we inherit our fortune. Consequently, real faith demonstrates self-denial, temperance or patience, and unreserved obedience; hard to find in our so-called Christian society. For genuine dominion, we need God's faith; the faith that flows through you as you hear and obey the voice of God. Faith that sees what God sees. This is a different ball game! It takes time to achieve and develop. That is why Adam spent time learning from God before Eve was made. The reason why Paul spent time in Arabia before his ministry became prominent; the reason why Jesus' ministry started at thirty instead of ten. They had to learn dominion. Let me give you an example. When God brought the people out of Egypt it was His purpose that they enter the Land of Promise. However, after forty years of meandering in the desert, they still did not enter. Why? Let God answer this one.

> "WHEREFORE, (AS THE HOLY GHOST SAITH, TODAY IF YE WILL HEAR HIS VOICE, HARDEN NOT YOUR HEARTS AS IN THE PROVOCATION, IN THE DAY OF TEMPTATION IN THE WILDERNESS. WHEN YOUR FATHERS TEMPTED ME, PROVED ME, AND SAW MY WORKS FORTY YEARS. *WHEREFORE I WAS GRIEVED WITH THAT GENERATION, AND SAID, THEY DO ALWAYS ERR IN THEIR HEART; AND THEY HAVE NOT KNOWN MY WAYS.* SO I SWARE IN MY WRATH, THEY SHALL NOT ENTER INTO MY REST.)" (HEBREWS 3:7-11)

The people of God refused to exercise faith, although they had seen the demonstration of God's power. God wanted to take them into the Promised Land of prosperity, but they couldn't believe His awesome power. God's faith is simply acting on what He has told you. And yes, this takes courage especially when your natural senses, the flesh and the devil are barking in your ears to the contrary. But you must take courage and exercise dominion.

When God first gave me the understanding of dominion, I kept hearing in my spirit, "I will make the people 'bread' (food) for you." Then, a few days after that, I got several tests in understanding dominion. One particular test the Lord gave me was from a man who I had intended to purchase a used car from for resale. He told me that he would charge me a fee on any car he would purchase for me to resell. At that time, I didn't have the money to pay the fee. So, I had no intention of going to get the car. But the Spirit of God told me to go forward and get the car. When I went to the office the fee was cancelled. God is sovereign, He can make the people into bread! (Not literal bread, of course, but the very people who may be your enemy...he can cause them to bless you!)

Many times instead of walking in confidence and dominion, we allow the devil to sap our courage. Dominion always has risks and dangers. These can only be surmounted if we "take courage." My brother Dave usually uses this expression when he is trying to comfort and motivate people: "take courage." Taking courage means we face our difficulty with the assurance that God will work it out. True courage is **rage** under the **control** of the Spirit. It's turning off the self-preservation and self-centered modes in our psyche and moving forward with faith and conviction under the inspiration of the Holy Spirit regardless of the costs. This is the only way to bring the abundance of both temporal and spiritual prosperity.

To the newcomer, dominion is reckless abandonment to the Spirit of God. It's doing crazy things in the Spirit. However, to those who have matured, dominion is walking in faith and love. We have come to love the Father so much that every breath that is drawn is done to please Him! Dominion is the essence of life and power in the Spirit, the power that angels flock around and from which demons flee.

This is what Jesus strived to teach His "faithless" disciples who constantly cowered in the face of adversity. Their eyes were blinded to the unlimited and irresistible power of God that cannot be withstood. Instead of stepping forward in childlike faith, they allowed their analytical minds to dominate them. But we must free ourselves from this bondage of pride that wants to exalt itself against the knowledge of God and bring every thought into the captivity of Christ. Jesus is the power of the universe. He holds it together by His word. This is the unadulterated truth. This will bring prosperity in every area of life.

FOR MORE INFORMATION:

VISIT US ON THE WORLD WEB:
WWW.MARRIAGEMECHANICS.ORG

EMAIL:
MARRIAGEMECHANICS@HOTMAIL.COM

OTHER BOOKS AVAILABLE

Her Feminine Side

The Price of Dominion

Fight For Your Marriage

Understanding Why We Fuss & Fight

Victory in the Bedroom

Cancer Doesn't Scare Me Anymore

Living Single

Overcoming Jezebel, Delilah, and Anger

The Whole Truth about Marriage, Divorce & Remarriage

The Treasure Box (Devotional)

Lord, Send a Revival!

The Noah Chronicles

DO YOU FEEL INADEQUATE AS A MAN?

ARE YOU UNSURE WHAT YOUR ROLE IS?

DO YOU TRULY UNDERSTAND WHAT GENDER EQUALITY MEANS?

DO YOU REALLY UNDERSTAND HOW AUTHORITY REALLY WORKS?

These and other pertinent questions are addressed and answered in Lambert Sands' newest work "Understanding Male Authority." In a time when patriarchy is scorned and considered outdated; where manhood, masculinity and fatherhood are challenged; and false equality is being paraded as evolved truth, "Understanding Male Authority" defines the male's role from a biblical perspective.

Blinded and confused by what is said in the media and social circles, most men have given up on being leaders. Even in the church, the keys of male and divine authority have been lost in our generation. Very often, we see the two extremes of leadership in operation. We see either male arrogance born out of insecurity and fear, or we see the spirit of the compromiser desperately trying to appease and avoiding confrontation; neither will bring deliverance nor elevate a man.

But, like scripture says, "When the enemy shall come in like a flood, the Spirit of the LORD shall lift up a standard against him." In this book, Lambert Sands points men to their true purpose and digs up a gem and the forgotten principle that draws God's favor and wisdom. Without it, men will continue to fail as leaders.

ABOUT THE AUTHOR

Lambert Sands is the President of Marriage Mechanics Ministries, Intl. He is originally from the Bahamas and is an ordained minister. He has been in ministry for forty years. He is a gifted speaker and author of numerous books. He currently lives in Orlando, Florida with his two daughters after the passing of his wife in 2012.